Curiosities of
—GREATER—
MANCHESTER

ROBERT NICHOLLS

06₁

First published in 2004 by
Sutton Publishing Limited · Phoenix Mill
Thrupp · Stroud · Gloucestershire · GL5 2BU

09348805 ✗

British Library Cataloguing in Publication Data
A catalogue record for this book is available from the British Library.

ISBN 0-7509-3661-4

To Patrick and Adrian

Typeset in 10/12 pt Palatino.
Typesetting and origination by
Sutton Publishing Limited.
Printed and bound in England by
J.H. Haynes & Co. Ltd, Sparkford.

CONTENTS

Visiting the Curiosities   4

Introduction   5

Acknowledgements   7

Map   8

1. City of Manchester   9
2. Salford   63
3. Trafford   77
4. Stockport   91
5. Tameside   111
6. Oldham   133
7. Rochdale   145
8. Bury   155
9. Bolton   165
10. Wigan   175
11. Curiosities that have now disappeared   185

Index   190

VISITING THE CURIOSITIES

Most of the curiosities listed in this book are not tourist attractions in their own right but can been seen, externally at least, without paying an admission fee. Many are visible from the public highway or from other freely accessible areas. A few have interiors where access might require payment of an admission charge. Where access is not possible, this is made quite clear in the 'Access' details given in the text.

The curiosities can be visited either singly, or in groups by area. Those in central Manchester are best visited on foot; others make ideal car outings. Most can be visited by public transport, and most can be seen by the less abled.

INTRODUCTION

When the idea of putting together a book on the oddities and curiosities of Greater Manchester was first suggested, I have to admit being somewhat reluctant at first to take on the task. This was because most of the excellent books on such matters, either on a national or regional basis, have tended to steer clear of the nation's big cities, and feature country areas or picturesque small-to-medium-sized towns of some tourist or visitor appeal.

As a result, many of these publications deal with natural features or curious little buildings from the past, often associated with an interesting story. No similar book on Greater Manchester, one of the most heavily built-up and continually developing areas in the UK, could hope to find the same volume of similar material.

In this I have been pleasantly proved wrong. Not only has Greater Manchester a large number of oddities and curiosities, it has a great range of them, dating from the prehistoric to man-made curiosities of recent times. Arguably, that range is far wider than that of the more rural shire counties, where books on the subject rarely contain references to twentieth-century sites.

The rural fringes of the county do indeed contain many examples of curiosities found in the shire counties. There are natural features, prehistoric earthworks, village stocks and wayside crosses in some quantity. Some of these can also be found in the built-up areas, often surviving, surprisingly, the effects of many generations of development and redevelopment. The Industrial Revolution in which the county played such a large part has left many curiosities. The post-industrial era of recent times has produced many fine examples of its own, although they may not yet be recognised as such in the public's eye.

Manchester was the world's first industrial city, leading the world in many things and providing the model of an emerging industrial society. Not surprisingly, many of its curiosities are associated with claims or records. The city and its hinterland was the destination of the first wholly artificial canal and main-line railway, and possessed Europe's fastest-growing airport. It continues to be the home of the UK's first free public library, the first public parks, and was the place where the first Nuclear Free Zone was declared. The Trades Union Congress first met in Manchester, and the Votes for Women movement had its origins in the city. It has the largest Education Precinct in the UK. In the areas of science and engineering it was where the first stored programme computer was built, where the atom was first split, and where the first industrial estate was located. The largest brick-built engineering structure, the largest Moravian settlement, the largest public air raid shelters outside London, the birthplace of the Co-operative movement, etc., etc.

The list is endless. All these happened within the boundaries of Greater Manchester.

'Greater Manchester' of course was an artificial creation. As an administrative county it lasted a mere twelve years. Many will argue that as a true 'county' it does not and never did exist. In an area where the regional accents change discernibly every 5 miles or so, the nature of the curiosities will vary too from district to district, and to a degree reflect the nature of the areas in which they are located. Although the City of Manchester naturally predominates, the contribution of each district of the so-called county is distinctive and makes up a satisfying total. Within those artificial boundaries lies an immense variety and richness of history, humanity and architecture, both past and present, which is reflected in the curiosities of the area.

The new millennium has seen the Greater Manchester area embarking on a fresh round of its development and evolution, in which the pace of change will vastly surpass all the previous generations of change that have gone before. This process of change will destroy some curiosities, create new ones and perhaps highlight our awareness and appreciation of the remainder, many of which form the collection to be found in the pages of this book.

The choice of curiosities that follow in these pages is inevitably a personal one. Readers will find many others.

ACKNOWLEDGEMENTS

Books of this nature can only be written with the willing assistance of a great many people.

Much information has been garnered from visits to the local history libraries at Manchester, Bury, Salford, Stockport, Tameside and Walkden. The pages of other books, guidebooks, the internet, tourist and publicity material produced over the years have also been useful sources of information, and thanks are due to the various authors who have allowed me to adapt their material for use in this book, especially Jonathan Schofield.

Innumerable land and property owners need to be thanked for giving me permission to enter their properties and allowing me to take photographs for the purpose of this book. The staff and clergy at the various churches deserve particular thanks in this regard.

Special thanks are also due to Chris Makepeace for help with obtaining certain historical material, to Ian Howarth of Manchester Airport for assistance with some of the photographs and to the Royal Exchange Theatre for the photograph on p. 15. John McDermott gave valuable assistance about Hulme's Bridge Ferry and the staff and the 'regulars' at the Cock Hotel, Worsley, should be mentioned for pointing me in the right direction over 'Polly the Pig'. Neil Richardson and Sue Steer also gave help on various matters.

Simon Fletcher at Sutton Publishing should be thanked for being such a willing advocate of the project and for helping me to realise it after so long.

Finally, thanks to my wife and family for tolerating another of my 'projects' which has taken up so much of my time.

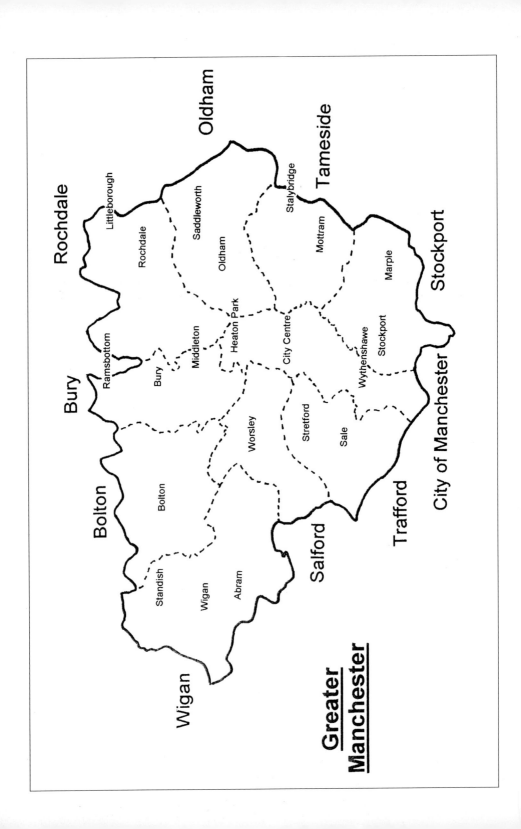

Greater Manchester

1

CURIOSITIES
OF THE CITY OF MANCHESTER

THE ALBERT MEMORIAL

Albert Square

Access

In the centre of
Albert Square,
next to the Town
Hall.

Manchester's Albert Memorial, designed by the notable Victorian architect, Thomas Worthington, pre-dates its neighbour the Town Hall and its larger and better known counterpart in London's Kensington Gardens, for which it is said to have been the model.

The memorial was built in 1867 in response to a memorial fund launched after the death of the Prince Consort in 1861. A fund committee was set up and initially looked at other ideas for a suitable memorial, but Worthington's design of a ciborium was finally chosen as being fortuitously suitable to house a statue of the Prince that had already been commissioned from Matthew Noble by the Mayor, Alderman Thomas Goadsby.

Below: The memorial in 1895.

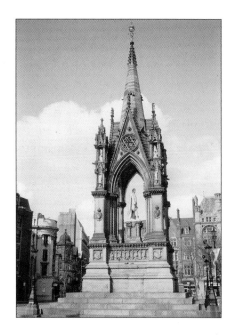

Prince Albert was a strong advocate of the need for industrial progress, and had always been well liked in Manchester. The whole of the memorial therefore contains elaborate sculptural representations of subjects in which he had an interest such as art, commerce, science and agriculture, together with the heads of great artists and composers, and the royal arms and crests of England and Saxony.

The Memorial has not always found a place in Manchester's heart, and suggestions were made some years ago that it be removed and sold. However, public generosity rescued it through the efforts of a trust, which arranged for its restoration and cleaning in the late 1970s, and its place in the Square is assured.

See also the magnificent gothic Town Hall, designed by Alfred Waterhouse, especially the Great Hall with its Ford Madox Brown mural paintings of famous events in Manchester's history. Free tours of the building, arguably one of the finest civic buildings in the country, are available most Wednesdays and Saturdays from the Visitor Information Centre.
Also in the Square is Worthington's Thirlmere Fountain, built in 1897 to celebrate the completion of the Thirlmere water supply scheme. The fountain was restored to its original site in the Square in 1998 after spending a period in Heaton Park.

THE HIDDEN GEM

Access

St Mary's Church, Mulberry Street

Close to Albert
Square, off
Brazenose Street.
The church is
open 9–5.30
every day except
Sunday.

This Catholic church has long been known as the 'Hidden Gem'.
Built in 1848, it replaced an earlier church on the site from 1794,
said to have been the first Catholic church to be built as a church
since the Reformation in any major English centre of population.

Until recently it had a comparatively unknown location, being in a small side street. Its rather plain exterior conceals an ornate yet compact interior, with highly decorated altarpiece and life-sized statuary, which is perhaps its true surprise. The building has an unusual spire, based on German medieval examples, and a top-lit interior. The Victorian architect Augustus Pugin, however, did not approve of the design.

One visiting Catholic bishop is reputed to have said, 'No matter what side of the church you look, you behold a hidden gem.'

The noted, but now almost-forgotten Italian tenor, Beniamino Gigli (1890–1957), led the singing at Mass here during a visit to Manchester in the late 1940s. Would today's 'celebrity' tenors do this?

In 1993–4 the church was completely restored, and in 1995 some graphic and eye-opening paintings of the Stations of the Cross, by Norman Adams RA, were commissioned by the parish priest Father Denis Clinch.

WHEN COTTON WAS KING

Cotton Trading Boards, Royal Exchange Theatre

Access

The theatre foyer is open most shopping days. The main entrance is from St Ann's Square.

It is increasingly being forgotten that Manchester was once 'Cottonopolis', the centre of cotton spinning and trading within the UK. At its peak in the 1830s it is said that the trade in cotton amounted to 50 per cent of total British exports.

The Royal Exchange was the place where cotton was bought and sold commercially, and the growth and decline of the exchange mirrored this expansion and decline. The first exchange was established in 1729 by Sir Oswald Mosley, and over the next two centuries there were successive expansions and re-buildings. The current building, which dates from 1874, lost its elaborate colonnaded frontage prior to the First World War, and was remodelled in 1920–1.

By the late 1920s total membership was about 11,000, and trading would take place in the Great Hall every Tuesday and Friday. Various claims were made about the Exchange – that it

was the 'largest trading room in the world', the 'eighth wonder of the world' and the 'hub of the universe'. The building was severely damaged by bombing in the Second World War. When reconstruction was completed in November 1953 the size of the main trading hall had been reduced by a third, reflecting the by then declining state of the industry. Final closure came on the last day of December 1968.

The trading boards (p. 14), high above the floor of the theatre, showing the prices of the different types of cotton, have been left exactly as they were when cotton trading finally ceased.

Following closure of the exchange the trading floor lay unused until it was developed imaginatively as the Royal Exchange Theatre between 1973 and 1976. The theatre structure itself, a true 'theatre in the round', looks rather like the Lunar Module of the Apollo space missions of that era, and is supported by the great columns that line the old trading hall. After the building suffered damage in the 1996 IRA bomb blast various improvements were undertaken, and the main theatre, which reopened in November 1998, now seats over 750.

THE LUCKIEST POST-BOX IN MANCHESTER

Access

Located close to the junction of Corporation Street and St Mary's Gate.

Victorian Post-Box, Corporation Street

This solid-looking Victorian post-box, built by Handysides of Derby, is usually unnoticed by the many thousands of shoppers, office workers and others who pass it every day.

On 15 June 1996 it acquired the status of being the luckiest post-box in Manchester by being sited only yards away from the vehicle that contained the huge (3,500lb) IRA terrorist bomb that devastated large areas of the city centre. The bomb has been claimed to be the largest peacetime bomb that has exploded in a British city since the Second World War.

By great good fortune no one was killed or seriously injured, but some £700 million worth of damage to property was done and some 670 businesses had to relocate. The buildings adjoining the post-box, dating from the 1950s, '60s and '70s (the old Marks & Spencer store, parts of the Arndale Centre and the 'British Engine' office block), were devastated.

The post-box, however, seemed to be in the epicentre of the blast, and suffered no more than a few minor scratches. A few days after the explosion a postman was allowed to pick his way through the surrounding debris to retrieve the post from inside the box and send it on its way.

Subsequently the post-box has been repainted and relocated slightly to tie in with the redevelopment of the surrounding area, being brought into use on its new site on 22 November 1999.

Something of an urban legend has grown around the box since 1996. If you want to be sure of your post getting to its destination, and other means of communication simply will not do, then this is *the* box to use.

Here are two views of the box, before the blast and as it is today.

THE LARGEST MARKS & SPENCER STORE IN THE WORLD

New Marks & Spencer's building

Access

On St Mary's Gate.

The extensive damage caused by the IRA terrorist bomb of 1996 gave the city an opportunity to redevelop the area. The results of this initiative, led by the Manchester Millennium consortium, a joint venture between the City Council and the private sector, and incorporating an international design competition, have been dramatic.

Within the area bounded by St Mary's Gate, Corporation Street, Cateaton Street and Deansgate, a number of new developments have been created. One of the first to be completed, in December 1999, was this £85 million new building for Marks & Spencer, whose previous building, dating from the 1950s and '60s, had to be demolished. For a time this was the largest Marks & Spencer store in the world, the store having four trading floors each the size of a football pitch.

This claim is now out of date, as the store proved too large for the trading conditions, and the building was subsequently split in two, with a new branch of Selfridges occupying the remainder of the building.

Although Marks & Spencer were first established in Leeds with a market stall, Manchester was the site of the chain's first real store, which opened in 1894.

While in the area have a look at Barton Arcade, just off St Ann's Square, a glazed shopping arcade dating from 1871, occasionally described as 'Manchester's Crystal Palace'.

THESE PUBLIC HOUSES HAVE BEEN MOVED TWICE

Access

On Exchange
Square.

The Old Wellington Inn and Sinclairs

These two pubs, collectively known as 'The Shambles', have been moved twice in the last three decades.

The Old Wellington Inn is one of Manchester's oldest buildings, dating from about 1550, although earlier claims have been made. It was the birthplace of John Byrom, poet, wit and writer of the hymn 'Christians Awake'. It became a pub in 1830, although for many years in the nineteenth century its upper floors were used by an optician and mathematical instrument maker.

Sinclair's Oyster Bar dates from 1738 and is said to have been one of the earliest gentlemen's clubs in the city. Its interior is full of nooks and crannies, and may have been the place where the

expression 'Mind your Ps and Qs' originated, from the days when one John Shaw was publican. One of his brews was so strong that you were only allowed to drink one pint if alone, and a quart if in the company of others.

When the area between St Mary's Gate and Cateaton Street was being redeveloped in the early 1970s both buildings had to be raised by 4ft 9in to fit in with the new buildings being built around them. The legal consequences of this were still being ironed out by all concerned well into the 1980s.

In 1996 the immediate buildings were devastated by the IRA bombing of the city centre, and it was decided to clear the entire site for completely new buildings.

The Shambles, however, was saved, and was transported across Cateaton Street to a site near the Cathedral, where the two buildings now form an L-shape. They were reopened in late 1999.

The two photographs show the buildings in their original and current locations.

THE OLDEST FREE PUBLIC REFERENCE LIBRARY IN THE UK

Chetham's Library, Long Millgate

Access

Located close to Victoria station, the library is open to readers and researchers, 9.00 am–12 noon/ 1.30–4.30 pm, though an appointment is necessary. Tours of the Library and other parts of the Chetham's complex are available each Wednesday afternoon after the free public concerts during school terms, although booking is necessary.

Chetham's Hospital, containing both the School of Music and Chetham's Library, is in one of Manchester's oldest buildings, deservedly with Grade I listed building status. Originally the manor house of Thomas de la Warre, it was given to the newly established Collegiate Church (later the Cathedral) in 1421 to become a Collegiate College.

Both School and Library were established in 1653 under the will of Humphrey Chetham, a wealthy Manchester merchant whose statue can be seen in the nearby Cathedral. The School was originally a Bluecoat School 'for the sons of honest, industrious and painful parents'. 'Chets', as it is sometimes called, has been a specialist co-educational music school since 1969, and has built up a superb reputation.

The Library is the oldest free public reference library in the UK and contains a wealth of historical material, particularly relating to the North-West. The library's Old Reading Room contains this attractive alcove, said to have been used by Harrison Ainsworth when writing his novels, and also to have been the meeting place of Karl Marx and Frederick Engels in 1845.

See also the remains of Hyde's Cross in the schoolyard, close to the Library entrance. Manchester's other central libraries are also housed in notable buildings. The Central Reference Library in St Peter's Square is located in a large circular structure, its main Social Sciences Library being slightly reminiscent of the old British Museum Reading Room. It is the largest municipal library in the UK.

The Portico Library on Mosley Street is in a Grecian-style building, while the University's John Rylands Library on Deansgate is housed in a cathedral-like late gothic edifice by Basil Champneys built in 1899.

A CURIOUS REMNANT OF A BRIDGE

Hanging Bridge

This curious remnant is the old Hanging Bridge, one of Manchester's oldest structures. This bridge, which has two arches built of local red Collyhurst sandstone, was probably built in the fifteenth century to cross the now covered-in Hanging Ditch, a deep (some say man-made) ravine said to have carried the mythical River Dene (from where the name Deansgate is said to originate), which flowed towards the River Irwell at this point.

Hanging Ditch was finally filled in *c.* 1770, and the bridge was half-hidden under the raised street level of Deansgate until it was

uncovered as part of the development of the Cathedral's new Visitor Centre, which opened in 2002.

The photograph above shows the bridge during an earlier uncovering at the start of the twentieth century.

The interior of the Cathedral is also well worth a visit. Reputedly, it has the widest nave in the country. There are impressive modern stained glass windows by Anthony Holloway and Margaret Traherne, as well as intricate carvings in wood and stone. The latter include a 'rebus' or a medieval joke. This is located over the entrance to the Lady Chapel, where there are small sculpted scenes of hunting and wine barrels, formerly called 'tuns'. These images relate to the name of the first warden of the Cathedral, called John Huntington.

A MAP OF WHERE THE TRAINS USED TO GO

Between
Deansgate and
Corporation
Street, with the
main passenger
entrances on
Long Millgate
and Todd Street.

Lancashire and Yorkshire Railway Map, Victoria station

Manchester's second busiest railway station is now largely robbed of its long-distance trains, and has had fewer trains serving it since changes were made to the railway system around Manchester a couple of decades ago, although it is now also served by the Metrolink tram/light rail system. The station has also shrunk in size, since part of its site was taken for the building of the Manchester Evening News Arena development in the 1990s.

Despite this the remaining parts have some interesting features. In the Booking Hall is this pre-1922 map of the old Lancashire & Yorkshire Railway Company's system. Beneath it is a large war memorial incorporating St George and St Michael.

See also, within the station, the ticket booths with their old enamel 'In' and 'Out' signs, the station buffet with its distinctively coloured glazed domed roof, and the glass canopy outside with the names of all the destinations once served by rail from the station.

The station also boasted the longest platform in the country. Until 1969 the former Platform 11 (now Platform 3) continued into the now closed adjacent Exchange station, with a total platform length of 2,194ft.

WHERE FISH USED TO BE TRADED

Old Smithfield Market

Access

At the northern
end of High
Street, or
alternatively via
the pedestrian
route through
the old market
from Shudehill.

These ornate frontages are the surviving part of Manchester's
former Wholesale Fish Market, which operated on this site
until the entire Smithfield Market complex moved to Openshaw
in 1973.

Built in 1873, the Wholesale Fish Market features ornate iron-
work and these carved bas-reliefs by Bonehill showing fishermen
casting their nets at sea.

Most of the Smithfield area is now a car park, but the former
fish market now houses a garden in part of its area. Across the
road is a surviving end façade of the old Retail Fish Market, built
in 1890, which lasted a few years longer than the wholesale
market. Part of this was subsequently developed by the local
authority as the highly successful Smithfield Craft Centre,
with studios, workshops, shops and galleries, in which use it
remains today.

A REMNANT OF MANCHESTER'S HYDRAULIC POWER SYSTEM

Access

Off Bridge Street, on the bank of the River Irwell, opposite the Mark Addy pub. There is a small fee payable on most days for going round the museum.

The Pump House, Water Street

This building, dating from 1909, is the sole survivor of Manchester's three hydraulic pumping stations, the huge iron water tanks on its roof giving a clue to its previous use.

Hydraulic power, a Victorian innovation, was utilised in many city centres and dock areas to power lifts, presses and forges, etc. The power from this station was responsible, among other things, for working the clock in the Town Hall and for raising the curtain at the city's Opera House. The power was transmitted by a system of iron pipes laid underground.

The spreading use of electricity caused a gradual decline in the use of hydraulic power, but the Manchester system, operated by the Corporation's Waterworks Department, did not close down until 1972.

For two decades the Water Street building was used by the College of Building, which formerly adjoined the site, but it then became the home of the National Museum of Labour History, called the Pump House People's History Museum.

Other small-scale remnants of the Manchester hydraulic power system can be found within the Greater Manchester Museum of Science and Industry.

ONCE PART OF SECRET MANCHESTER

Guardian Telephone Exchange, George Street

Access

George Street runs parallel to Mosley Street and Portland Street. The building is now partly hidden by the recently built Novotel.

This ugly building, completely without any exterior means of identification, is the main entrance and ventilation shaft serving the Manchester Guardian telephone exchange. This was constructed underground in the early 1950s by the Post Office during the atomic bomb era, when it was designed to enable the then telephone system to withstand a 20-kiloton Hiroshima-sized bomb dropped on the city centre.

The exchange, similar to systems built at the same time in London and Birmingham, comprises a system of tunnels running beneath buildings in Back George Street, some 112ft deep, 1,000ft long and 25ft wide, with lengthy branches running out to Lockton Close in Ardwick, and Chapel Street in Salford.

Reports of the system describe it as having its own artesian well, generators, fuel tanks and rest rooms with artificial windows and scenery.

Publication of details of the system remained prohibited under the 'D notice' system until 1967, but it had been rendered obsolete by the development of the hydrogen bomb in 1955. It no longer forms part of the main British Telecom network, although it is believed to continue in use for private line networks.

ORIENTAL MANCHESTER

Chinese Arch, Faulkner Street

Access

'Chinatown' is
between Princess
Street, Mosley
Street, Portland
Street and York
Street. The arch
is at the lower
end of Faulkner
Street, close to
Dickinson Street.

This impressive arch, set in the heart of the city's 'Chinatown', was completed in 1987, and is said to be a token of friendship between the Chinese people and the city of Manchester. It is claimed to be the first true Imperial Chinese Arch in Europe.

The structure's concrete framework was erected by the former Greater Manchester Council, while its elaborate decoration was organised by the local Chinese community, who arranged for the materials used and the craftsmen who carried out the work to be brought over from China. A small Chinese garden has been laid out on the edges of the adjoining car park. The arch is the focal point of Chinatown and its construction firmly established the area as part of the city's rich cultural heritage.

The growth of Chinatown, virtually unknown as such in the 1960s when the area was still run-down textile warehouses, has been phenomenal. This first started with the opening of the original Kwok Man restaurant on George Street in the late 1960s, and was aided partly by the transfer to Manchester of many of Liverpool's long established Chinese community, and also by the investment of some of Hong Kong's wealth prior to the 1997 takeover by China itself. Manchester now has the largest Chinese population of any city in Europe and has been accorded the status of a Dragon City.

The best time to get a proper flavour of Chinatown is on a Sunday, or better still when the Chinese New Year is being celebrated.

MANCHESTER'S SMALLEST PUB

The Circus, Portland Street

Access

On Portland
Street, near to its
junction with
Princess Street.

This is reputedly the smallest public house in Manchester, although the Grey Horse a few doors away must also be a close contender. Sometimes the claim is modified to that of being the smallest serving bar area.

The pub is one of the oldest in Manchester and both it and the Grey Horse are named after Mr Handy's equestrian circus, which operated in a nearby building from 1793 to 1797.

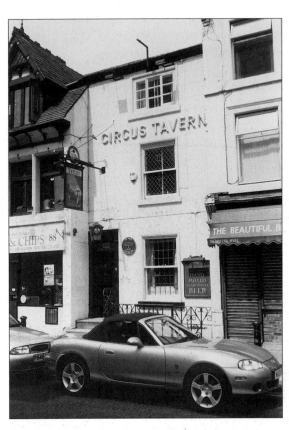

The drinking area is little more than two small rooms and a short corridor and only one person can stand behind the bar. There is a distinctly downmarket atmosphere and a welcome reluctance to change with the times that contrasts with many of the glass and chrome establishments of the revitalised city centre. 'Real ale' is served, and lager is a comparatively recent addition. On Saturday nights the front door is closed to keep out unwelcome revellers, but regulars can gain access via a second doorway from the rear street.

See also the former Mechanics' Institute at 103 Princess Street, where the first Trades Union Congress was held in 1868.

PINK MANCHESTER:
BRITAIN'S FIRST 'GAY VILLAGE'

Alan Turing Statue, Sackville Street

Access

Located in the small park at the junction of Sackville Street and Whitworth Street.

Manchester's 'Gay Village', reputedly the first in the UK, is located around Canal Street. Like Chinatown its growth has been rapid, although in this case rather more recent, particularly from 1988 to the early 1990s, when upmarket bars, cafés and clubs catering for the gay community began to spring up in the old warehouses that lined the Rochdale Canal. These were soon followed by gay bookshops, solicitors and other commercial outlets. To the regret of some the area has become more 'mixed' in recent years as mainstream breweries have taken over some of the establishments, and it has become fashionable with tourists.

Close by is this recent statue of Alan Turing by Glyn Hughes, completed in 2001 and cast in the Arts and Crafts Foundry in Tianjin, China.

Turing (1912–54) was educated at King's College, Cambridge, and in 1936 laid the foundations of modern computer science. During the Second World War he worked on code-breaking at Bletchley Park and devised the 'Bombe', the mechanical forerunner of today's computers. After the war he worked for Manchester University, which was where the first stored programme electronic computer was developed in 1948. An open homosexual, Turing was prosecuted for his activities in 1952 and committed suicide two years later.

The sculpture was the result of efforts made within the gay community, together with public subscriptions, and donations from the local authority and the British Society of Mathematicians.

WHERE VIMTO WAS FIRST BREWED

Vimto Sculpture, Granby Row

Access

On Granby Row, immediately behind the main UMIST building.

This sculpture, comprising a bottle and ingredients used in the brewing of the distinctive dark non-alcoholic drink, is called 'A Monument to Vimto'. It was created in stained oak by Kerry Morrison in 1992.

It is located on the site of 49 Granby Row, where John Joel Nichols (no relation to the author) mixed the first brew of Vimto in 1908.

The sculpture was commissioned by J.N. Nichols (Vimto) plc, a firm that is proud of its history but guards the recipe for its product with great vigour.

THE QUEEN OF MANCHESTER WAREHOUSES

Britannia Hotel, Portland Street

Access

Near the top end of Portland Street, close to the junction with Aytoun Street.

Originally known in the city as 'Watts's Warehouse', this building was erected on a whole city block in 1858, at a cost of £100,000, for the largest wholesale drapery business in the city. The older photograph (overleaf) shows it as it was in the latter half of the nineteenth century. James Watts, the proprietor, was the classic Manchester entrepreneur, the son of a self-made man, free trader and religious dissenter. It is said that Prince Albert stayed with him at his Abney Hall home in Cheadle when he opened the Art Treasures Exhibition in 1857.

Watts's warehouse exemplifies the confident spirit of its owner with its mixture of styles and detail. Close examination of the exterior reveals that each floor is given a different architectural treatment, starting with Egyptian at the bottom, and rising through Italian Renaissance, Elizabethan, French Renaissance and

Flemish. At the top the roof line is divided by four towers, each of which contains a number of large Gothic rose windows. Inside there is an impressive war memorial to employees killed in both world wars.

During the Second World War many warehouses in the area were destroyed by fires caused by incendiary bombs (the Piccadilly Plaza development was built on such a site), while others were designated to be demolished to prevent the fires spreading, including the S. & J. Watts building.

The owners had their own private fire brigade, led by Wilf Beckett, who refused to accept the decision of the authorities and resolved to save his employer's building. In 1940 during one such raid the authorities cut off the water supply to Beckett and his small band of volunteers but they successfully fought the fires that had started in the building using no more than blankets and sheets. The same team saved the building again in 1941. Beckett was subsequently honoured, on behalf of his team, at Buckingham Palace.

The business of S. & J. Watts became Cooke and Watts at a later date and finally closed down in 1972. The building was set to be converted into an office block when work was halted following a collapse of the property market in 1974. It remained untouched for a number of years, but its listed building status ensured that demolition was not an option. Since 1982 it has been the Britannia Hotel, and the status of this, the 'Queen of Manchester Warehouses', seems assured.

A GRAND ENTRANCE FOYER FOR AN OFFICE BLOCK

Entrance Hall, St James's Buildings

Access

On Oxford Street, next to the Palace Theatre.

This entrance hall must surely be the most impressive foyer to any office building in the city centre. Up to a decade or two ago the effect was complemented by the presence of uniformed commissionaires.

It is believed that the foyer was actually the entrance hall of an earlier building on the site, the St James Hall, where exhibitions, contests, and various entertainments were put on. The present building, with its impressive façade of Portland stone full of baroque detail, was built in 1912, and was built as the head office of the Calico Printers Association (or the CPA to older Mancunians), which was an amalgamation of many textile printing companies with mills all around Greater Manchester. It is claimed that the building has over 1,000 rooms.

The CPA itself was taken over by Tootal at the end of the 1960s and most of its former mills have closed. Its former head office became an office block.

THE BRIDGEWATER HALL 'PEBBLE'

'Touchstone', Barbirolli Square

Access

In the square, fronting the Bridgewater Hall, on Lower Mosley Street.

This kidney bean-shaped sculpture is called 'Touchstone' or 'Ishinki', and is by Kam Yasuda. It was placed here in 1996 at a cost of some £200,000, an amount which caused quite a stir at the time, although the costs were met by the Arts Council Lottery Fund and Manchester Airport who sponsored the project.

The stone was intended by its creator to introduce a natural shape into the sharply angular urban surroundings. Visitors certainly are drawn to it and often feel its smooth texture by

running their hands over it. Views are mixed as to whether this reflects its creator's intentions, or the mere wish to touch such an expensive piece of stone!

The Square also contains a bust of Sir John Barbirolli, the famous conductor of the Hallé Orchestra, who died in 1970.

The adjacent Bridgewater Hall, completed in September 1996, has at long last given Manchester a truly magnificent concert hall. The building (tours are available) is designed to prevent any outside noise, in particular the adjacent Metrolink trams, penetrating the main concert hall, which is supported on huge springs. Even the sound of the IRA bomb of June 1996 could not be heard by the workmen putting the finishing touches to the building.

THE 'LEAST INTERESTING ROMAN REMAINS IN ENGLAND'

Roman Wall, Castlefield

Access

Located underneath a railway arch close to Collier Street. Access to this is currently not possible.

Through the commendable efforts of the City Council and the former Central Manchester Development Corporation, the tourist potential of the Castlefield area has been developed. The area was designated as the UK's first Urban Heritage Park in 1982.

As part of this, two imitation stretches of wall from the former Roman fort of Castlefield have been built upon the original alignments of the fort's walls.

This section of wall, once described as 'the least interesting Roman remains in England', is a genuine section of the original fort. The fort had largely disappeared by the start of the nineteenth century, but sufficient of it remained for the Earl of Ellesmere, then the major landowner in the area, to hold up the building of the railway line to Altrincham until he had been satisfied that adequate measures had been taken to minimise the effects on the remains. He also insisted that the railway company provided castellated decorations to adorn the railway viaduct in the area, although today these seem an inappropriate reminder of the area's Roman past.

It is to be hoped that one day the authorities will be able to secure public access to this genuine relic of Roman Manchester.

THE BRIDGEWATER CANAL TERMINATED HERE

Grocers' Warehouse, Castlefield

Access

On Castle Street, just off Deansgate.

This interesting structure is one of the original termination points of the Bridgewater Canal. The canal first reached the area in 1764, but differences in level on the Manchester side of the canal meant that cargoes had to be raised up a considerable height to the level of the road on Castle Street.

To overcome this, James Brindley extended the canal in 1765 by driving it in a short tunnel under the street. A 47ft-deep shaft was then dug to link canal and street and a hoist was installed to allow the transfer of goods. The hoist was driven by a waterwheel fed with water from the canal.

By the 1770s a warehouse had been built over the structure. Initially known as the Gilbert & Henshall Warehouse (Hugh Henshall was Brindley's brother-in-law), it then became the Grocers' Warehouse after occupation by the Grocers' Company between 1811 and 1831.

The warehouse (or rather what was left of it) was finally demolished in 1960, although use of the hoist mechanism had ceased much earlier. In 1987 parts of the warehouse were rebuilt and a modified version of the hoist installed, as part of the development of the Castlefield area for tourism.

THE WORLD'S LONGEST RUNNING SOAP OPERA

Coronation Street set

Access

Visible only through the gates at the junction of Atherton Street and Great John Street. Public access to the Granada TV site is not allowed.

This street of what appears to be normal terraced housing is the set used by Granada TV for the shooting of outdoor scenes in the soap opera *Coronation Street*, or 'Corrie' as it has become known in recent years to its devotees. For a time public access to this was possible as the set formed part of the 'Granada Studios Tours' tourist complex which operated from the late 1980s for a decade or so.

The set is now full-sized but prior to 1988 an earlier set within the Granada TV site existed at two-thirds size. When the set was rebuilt detailed computer modelling was used by the designers to ensure that the changeover was not noticeable to the viewing public. The interior of the set is not used for shooting indoor scenes of the series, and comprises offices and storerooms.

Coronation Street is the world's longest running soap opera. Described as showing 'the everyday lives of ordinary folk', it was devised by Tony Warren and first transmitted on 9 December 1960. Employment on the show has been described as 'like working for local government' in view of the stable employment it can offer for many of its characters. It has been sold to over twenty-five countries around the world

and continues to be successful despite many competing examples of the genre.

While in the area see also Manchester's 'Harley Street': St John Street is an attractive Georgian and neo-Georgian street of doctors' surgeries and barristers' chambers.

THE WORLD'S OLDEST RAILWAY STATION

Liverpool Road station

Access

Now part of the Greater Manchester Museum of Science and Industry. The museum's main entrance is on Lower Byrom Street. It is open most days of the year and admission is free.

This modest-looking Georgian-style building is the oldest railway passenger station in the world. Opened on 15 September 1830 by the Prime Minister, the Duke of Wellington, together with the rest of the Liverpool and Manchester Railway, it remained in use for only fourteen years before it was replaced by Victoria station.

It was originally provided with separate booking halls for first- and second-class passengers, and passengers joined the trains at first floor level. No platforms were provided.

The building remained in use as a goods station until the early 1970s when moves began to be made for its preservation. The science museum eventually opened in 1983 and has expanded

considerably since. Among the other exhibits there is an interesting display on the history of the railway and station. At track level can be seen a sundial, a relic from the first years of operation, when it was used to record train arrival and departure times, as Manchester did not officially adopt 'Railway Time' until 1847.

The earlier photograph above shows the building in the early years of the twentieth century.

A RELIC FROM THE DAYS WHEN A MANCHESTER SUBURB HAD ITS OWN 'CONGESTION CHARGE'

Old Toll Gates, Victoria Park

Access

Located in the central grass island of Park Crescent, just off the eastern side of Wilmslow Road (A34) about 1½ miles south of the city centre.

These old castellated toll gateposts originally stood at the Daisy Bank Road entrance to the Victoria Park estate, as shown in the photograph opposite, taken in the early twentieth century. Victoria Park was promoted by a company acting under an Act of Parliament granted in 1837. Roads and sewerage were provided. Although development commenced, the company was bankrupt by 1839.

Many spacious villas were built privately in the years that followed and for a time in the nineteenth century the Park enjoyed a status as an affluent and exclusive suburb. In order to allow work to continue a trust was formed by residents in 1845; this assumed responsibility for the private roads within the Park,

including Anson Road, and charged tolls for their use, which also had the effect of keeping out unwanted traffic.

Changing economic and social patterns after 1900, the dubious legal status of the Victoria Park Trust, and longstanding antagonism towards the Trust from Manchester Corporation all contributed towards a long and marked decline for Victoria Park. Anson Road was taken over by the Corporation in 1938 but tolls for using the smaller Park roads continued until 1954, when the Trust was finally wound up and the roads formally adopted by the Corporation.

The toll gates shown on p. 42 were re-erected in 1987 in a joint scheme between the City Council and the local Civic Society to commemorate the 150th anniversary of the founding of the park. It was also one of a number of measures to restore some of the lost status of the Park, although since the photograph was taken the central replica toll notices have disappeared.

RELICS FROM MANCHESTER'S BLITZ OF 1940

On Lower
Ormond Street,
off Oxford Road.
The church is
open most days.

Montage, St Augustine's Church, All Saints

This metal montage, visible on one of the side walls inside this modern church completed in 1968, consists of the remains of the Sacred Vessels of two Catholic churches on Granby Row and York Street which were both destroyed in the Manchester Blitz of December 1940.

The montage was made by Robert Brumby, and the earliest of the vessels is said to date from before 1800.

See also while in the University area the small Geological Garden on Bridgeford Street. This forms part of the Manchester Museum. Also worth visiting is the Pankhurst Centre, on Nelson Street, originally the home of the leaders of the Suffragette movement.

A CHURCH BUILT TO AN 'ARTS AND CRAFTS' DESIGN

First Church of Christ, Scientist, Victoria Park

Access

On Daisy Bank Road, just off Anson Road.

This unusual church was built in 1903, being designed by the Manchester architect Edgar Wood (1860–1935). It was not part of the Victoria Park scheme, but has been described as 'a superb example of the avant-garde wing of the Arts and Crafts movement'. Nikolaus Pevsner has stated that it is 'one of the most original buildings of 1903 in England or indeed anywhere . . . indispensable in a survey of the development of the twentieth century church design in all England'.

The church itself closed for worship in December 1971, and the severe vandalism that followed nearly resulted in the loss of this fine listed building. However, it was saved at the last minute when the local authority stepped in three years later and bought the building. It was then successfully restored and became the Edgar Wood Centre, a drama and arts workshop run by the Manchester Polytechnic, later the Manchester Metropolitan University. The building was sold in 1998, and after a period of use for commercial purposes is currently vacant.

See also, virtually opposite, the attractive Addison Terrace. A blue plaque on one of the buildings commemorates two famous past residents – Charles Hallé (founder of the Hallé Orchestra) and the artist Ford Madox Brown.

ASIAN MANCHESTER

'Curry Mile', Oxford Road, Rusholme

Access

About 1½ miles
south of the city
centre on the
A34.

Dating from the 1960s and 1970s, but substantially extended recently with new developments, is Manchester's 'Curry Mile' (actually just over half a mile), a nickname bestowed on the area by passing students. Occasionally it is also referred to as 'Naanchester'.

Both sides of the road are lined with fluorescent neon-lit restaurants, sweet centres, travel agents, banks, jewellers and shops selling saris and other apparel from the Indian subcontinent. It is reputed to be the largest single concentration of Asian restaurants in the UK, and is said to be visited by some 10,000 customers each week. Unlike Chinatown, where a large proportion of diners are from the local Chinese community, the Curry Mile restaurants have a wider clientele.

The fifty or so restaurants are collectively known as Indian, but are much more likely to be serving Punjabi, Kashmiri, Persian, Bangladeshi and Nepalese food. The restaurants are constantly in a state of flux and change, but all offer very good value for money.

THE 'TOASTRACK BUILDING'

Hollings College, Wilmslow Road

Access

Located on Old Hall Lane, just off Wilmslow Road, between Rusholme and Fallowfield.

Known to generations of Manchester students as the 'Toastrack Building', or less commonly the 'Toastrack and Fried Egg Building', are the distinctive buildings of Hollings College.

A foundation stone on the building indicates that it was laid in 1958 by Sir Edward Boyle, then Minister for Education. The buildings later became part of the Manchester Polytechnic, now Manchester Metropolitan University. Appropriately they contain that University's Faculty of Food, Clothing and Hospitality Management.

While in the area, see also the 'Pot Church' or Holy Trinity Church on Platt Lane, so called because it is entirely clad in terracotta.

A FILLING STATION FOR HORSES

Drinking Trough, Copson Street, Withington

Access

At the junction
of Copson Street
and Hill Street.

This old drinking trough, standing on the edge of a small car park, used to stand at the junction of Wilmslow Road and Palatine Road. First erected in 1876, it was one of many provided on the city's streets when road traffic was horse-powered.

After being removed from its original site it languished in a farmer's field until being located here in the mid-1980s by the local Civic Society, in cooperation with the developers of the adjacent shopping centre.

ALSO KNOWN AS THE 'CALENDAR HOUSE'

The Towers, Wilmslow Road, Didsbury

Access

Located within
the grounds of
the Towers 2000
Business Park,
into which public
access is not
permitted.

This building, for a long time known as the Shirley Institute, was built in 1871 by the architect Thomas Worthington for John Taylor, proprietor and editor of the *Manchester Guardian*. Taylor sold it almost immediately to the industrialist Daniel Adamson, and it was in this building in 1882 that he hosted the crucial meeting of Manchester businessmen and civic leaders that led to the formation of the Manchester Ship Canal Company.

The building befitted its name, with its steep roofs, towers, turrets and acutely angled dormers. For a time it was known locally as the 'Calendar House', as it was believed to have 12 towers, 52 rooms and 364 windows.

In 1920 it became the Shirley Institute, and in the late 1980s the surroundings were developed as the Towers 2000 Business Park.

WHERE THE HOUSES HAD BOTH GAS AND ELECTRIC LIGHTING

Chorltonville

The garden suburb of Chorltonville is perhaps the best example of a number of 'garden suburbs' built in Greater Manchester (others exist at Burnage, Fairfield, Oldham and Alkrington).

It was finished in 1911, being opened on 7 October of that year by Harry Nuttall, MP for Stretford. It had a total area of 36 acres, and was provided with tennis courts, a bowling green, a children's playground and appropriate-sounding rural street names. The whole estate was the idea of two Manchester traders, Alderman James Herbert Dawson and William John Vowles, who both attended the Cavendish Chapel at All Saints. The scheme designer was Albert Cuneo.

The original plan was to provide decent homes for the inhabitants of the poorest areas of the city, but the project became more of a commercial proposition when the two founders joined

in partnership with a builder, a New Zealander called Thomas Whitely. A pilot scheme was undertaken in a different part of Chorlton.

Initially the Chorltonville houses were let to tenants with rents starting at £24 per annum, with tenants having to own at least two £5 shares in the estate company. However, after the First World War the company was wound up and the houses were then sold to the sitting tenants. No two houses on the estate are of the same design.

When the estate was first built houses lit by electricity were still a comparative rarity. The local gas supplier would not supply gas for cooking and heating only but insisted that the houses also be lit by gas. The estate company wanted electric lighting and the result was a curious compromise. The kitchens, sculleries and outhouses of the properties were lit by gas, with the remainder by electricity.

A REMINDER OF A VICTORIAN RAILWAY KING

Glacial Boulder, Rosehill, Northenden

Access

Off Longley
Lane, via
Bronington
Close.

This mushroom-like feature, sometimes called the 'Sharstone', is a glacial boulder located on a metal base shaped like a tree trunk. It was located in the grounds of Rosehill, once the home of Victorian railway magnate Sir Edward Watkin, and was placed here on what is said to be the old boundary between Northenden and Gatley in memory of Sir Edward's father, who had first bought the property.

Sir Edward was a friend of the political luminaries of the day, and it is said that both Gladstone and Disraeli visited Rosehill. Watkin was most notably chairman of the Great Central, Metropolitan and South Eastern Railway companies, which when linked together connected Manchester with one of his other ambitious projects, namely the Channel Tunnel.

Work had actually been started on the latter when the government of the day called it to a halt on the grounds that it would weaken national security. Sir Edward was involved in another ambitious but abortive project, to build a replica of the Eiffel Tower at Wembley, the site of which subsequently became Wembley Stadium.

There is a memorial to Sir Edward in Northenden Church. After his death Rosehill came into local authority ownership, being used as a hospital, orphanage and latterly as a remand home. In the early 1980s a famous painting, *The Icebergs* by Edwin Church, was discovered among its contents. The subsequent sale of the painting raised £3 million for the council.

Since closure of the remand home the grounds have been developed for private housing, and the home itself is currently being split into luxury flats, called Ashley Grange. These developments have resulted in a slight change to the location of the boulder, but it seems to have found a place at the heart of the new layout.

A MEMENTO FROM A WYTHENSHAWE FARMHOUSE

Access

On the western side of Greenbrow Road, Newall Green, which is to the west of junction 4 of the M56.

Knob Hall Gardens, Wythenshawe

The Wythenshawe estate was originally intended to be Britain's third Garden City after Letchworth and Welwyn Garden City. The Corporation engaged Barry Parker, the distinguished architect and associate of Ebenezer Howard, the originator of the Garden City movement and, some would say, of the town planning system itself, as their chief designer of the scheme.

Development of Wythenshawe started in the late 1920s but was interrupted by the start of the Second World War, and Parker himself retired in 1940. Subsequent development in the postwar period departed from the Garden City idea.

This small development dates from the 1950s and is unusual in that a small decorative ball was retained from Knob Hall, the farmhouse that had previously stood on the site.

For a good example of Parker's Wythenshawe (much of which has survived remarkably well), see the Mitchell's Gardens group of aged persons' dwellings on Hollyhedge Road, which was renovated a few years ago.

A Curious Garden close to the Airport

Memorial Garden, Woodhouse Lane, Heyhead

This curious little garden, sandwiched between two car parks at the airport, is all that remains of the former Heyhead Congregational Chapel, which was first built on this site in 1862, partly through the generosity of James Watts. The chapel was part of the hamlet of Heyhead, a market gardening settlement that survived the construction of the nearby Wythenshawe estate.

The continued expansion of the airport meant the end of Heyhead and the chapel was demolished in 1992. As a goodwill gesture the airport agreed to provide this small garden, containing memorial plaques from inside the chapel and its war memorials, which was incorporated into the landscaping of the car parks being built at the time.

Access

Adjacent to the footpath that links Ringway Road, Ringway Road West and Woodhouse Lane.

A MEMORIAL TO A LOCAL NATURALIST

Access

Off Mill Lane.

T.A. Coward Memorial, Cotterill Clough, Ringway

This stone memorial commemorates the Cheshire naturalist, Thomas Coward (1867–1933). Coward initially entered the family business but certain family members encouraged him to take up an interest in nature.

In the 1890s he began to contribute articles to magazines on the subject, and in 1900 his first book, *The Birds of Cheshire*, was published. From then on his contribution to the subject was prolific, with numerous books, and regular articles in the *Manchester Guardian*. From 1916 to 1919 he was acting Keeper of the Manchester Museum and served on its Committee for many years.

Cotterill Clough was a favourite haunt of his (he was born in nearby Bowdon), and after his death an appeal was launched to secure its long-term preservation. This was successful and the site is now designated as a Site of Special Scientific Interest.

HOW LOCAL GOVERNMENT USED TO BE ORGANISED IN MANCHESTER

Old Town Hall, Stockport Road, Levenshulme

This building, now the Levenshulme Antiques Village, is a relic of the way local government was organised in Manchester in the late nineteenth century.

Manchester Corporation, newly established in 1838, controlled a relatively small area, comprised of only the central areas of the city as it is today. Outlying areas were under the control of their own Local Boards or (later) Urban District Councils. The buildings of such authorities are sometimes still in existence, as here in Levenshulme, other examples being in Longsight, Withington and Cheetham.

Gradually between 1885 and 1909 the smaller authorities voted for incorporation into Manchester, mainly because amalgamation with the larger body enabled them to gain advantages for services such as water supply, sewerage and health provision.

Bearing a foundation stone dated 5 February 1898, the building was put up for the Levenshulme Urban District Council. Some of its lower floor windows until recently still bore the initials L.U.D.C. in etched glass. Its use as a town hall was short-lived, as Levenshulme became part of Manchester in 1909.

It became the Antiques Hypermarket in the late 1970s after serving as a Social Services Area Office.

REMAINS OF AN EARLY SWEDENBORGIAN CHURCH

The Round House, Every Street, Ancoats

This curious circular structure is the remains of the Round House, first erected in 1821 by the radical doctor and Swedenborgian minister, James Scolefield. The stone inscribed 'Christ Church', now facing east in part of the remaining wall, was originally located over the entrance doorway, as can be clearly seen on the earlier photograph opposite. The building was the location of a Chartist convention in 1842.

In the 1920s the building was taken over by the Manchester University Settlement, a charitable body set up by individuals from the university in the 1890s to undertake work in the poorer districts of the city. The Settlement remained in the building until the early 1970s, when the threat of a road scheme (which,

incidentally, was never carried out) obliged them to relocate to Beswick. After being vacated the building was badly vandalised and was then largely demolished, leaving only the present landscaped structure as a token reminder.

MANCHESTER'S 'FENIAN ARCH'

Railway Bridge, Hyde Road, West Gorton

Access

On Hyde Road
(A57), about
1 mile east of the
city centre.

Located at the point where the main Manchester to London railway line crosses Hyde Road is what older generations of Mancunians call the 'Fenian Arch'. It gained this name following an attack by a crowd of Irishmen on 18 September 1867 on a police van carrying two Fenian prisoners, Kelly and Deasy, to the (now long demolished) Belle Vue Jail.

During the attack, in which the prisoners were released, Police Sergeant Brett was killed. In the aftermath three of the attackers, Allen, Larkin and O'Brien were arrested. The evidence that any of them had fired the fatal shot was flimsy but the authorities were determined to see the matter through and all three were hanged at the New Bailey Jail, formerly located on Bridge Street. This is said to have been the last public execution in the UK.

The original archway has long gone, since the railway was subsequently widened, and the whole bridge was rebuilt in 1959 when the railway was electrified.

In St Joseph's Cemetery, Moston Lane, a large Celtic cross called the Martyrs' Memorial commemorates Allen, Larkin and O'Brien.

A MYSTERIOUS EARTHWORK

Nicko Ditch, Gorton

Access

Good stretches are to be found in Gorton Cemetery, Platt Fields Park, and this stretch between Holmcroft Road and Mount Road, Gorton.

Sometimes called the Great, Nicko or Mickle Ditch, this mysterious man-made earthwork, running (where it survives) from Platt Fields Park in the south of the city, to Ashton Moss in the east, has puzzled many as to its true origin. Some authorities have argued that it extended further westwards into Stretford, possibly as far as Salford.

One theory holds that it was dug in a single night in AD 923 as a defensive earthwork against the Danes by Mercian forces under the command of King Edward. Others suggest that it was some sort of manorial or ownership boundary, and this is the most favoured explanation today. Even its date of construction is obscure, and excavations carried out at various locations between 1990 and 1997 were unable to help solve the riddle. Much of the ditch has been submerged beneath later urban development.

MANCHESTER'S ORIGINAL TOWN HALL FRONTAGE

Heaton Park

Access

Heaton Park has four main entrances. The closest to this curiosity is the Grand Lodge entrance, at the corner of Bury Old Road and Sheepfoot Lane.

This colonnaded façade came from Manchester's original Town Hall, which stood at the corner of Cross Street and King Street. Designed by Francis Goodwin, the Town Hall (shown on the engraving opposite) was built for the local Police Commissioners between 1822 and 1825, at a total cost of £25,000.

In 1838, following the passing of the Municipal Corporations Act and a bitterly fought campaign by Richard Cobden MP, Manchester obtained its first modern democratically elected administration. The new corporation did not, however, gain immediate access to the Town Hall, constructed by the old administration, which barred access and obliged the new corporation to meet in an adjoining public house for a period of two years.

The King Street building was replaced by the present Town Hall, built between 1868 and 1877, following which it then served as the main public reference library until 1911, when the City Council decided to demolish it. Public opposition to the plan, particularly from a group of architects led by Edgar Wood, led to a decision to retain the façade. Platt Fields Park was considered as a possible location but was rejected after public opposition, following which the façade was erected in Heaton Park, close to the boating lake.

See also within the park the circular Summer House (near the Hall), the remains of the Dower House (currently being restored and extended) and the Telecom Tower. Heaton Park is reputedly the largest municipal park in the UK.

A PART OF MANCHESTER'S ORIGINAL TRAMWAY SYSTEM

Heaton Park Tramway, Middleton Road

Access

The tramway
runs between
the park's
Middleton Road
entrance and the
boating lake. It is
operated on
summer Sundays
and Bank
Holidays.

Britain's town and cities are once again developing tramways and other light rapid transit rail systems as part of the solution to the nation's increasing traffic problems. Manchester led the way with the development of its Metrolink system, the first section of which opened in 1992.

It is often forgotten that an earlier generation of tramway systems serving these same cities was discontinued as tramways were felt to be contributing toward traffic congestion. Manchester's own system ended in 1949.

This short length of tramway is operated by the Manchester Transport Museum Society. Unlike other tramway museums, the track here incorporates a stretch of genuine former Manchester Corporation Tramways alignment, originally constructed in 1905. After being abandoned in 1934 this track was covered over and largely forgotten about until the line was reopened by the Society in 1979. It has been extended to the boating lake since.

A number of single-deck tramcars are operated, one of which is a rare surviving Manchester vehicle, a 'California' car that used to run on the city's lengthy No. 53 circular route.

2

CURIOSITIES OF SALFORD

A NINETEENTH-CENTURY PUBLIC HERO

Mark Addy public house, Bridge Street

This pub, opened in August 1981 by local bookmaker and entrepreneur Jim Ramsbottom, is named after a famous nineteenth-century oarsman who rescued over 50 people from the dirty waters of the River Irwell. Addy was the only civilian to receive the Albert Medal (the predecessor of the Victoria Cross), which was awarded to him in 1878, when he saved 36 lives. His last rescue was in 1889, after which he contracted tuberculosis and died a year later, at 51.

The river level area was known as the New Bailey landing stage, and was the main boat-passenger waiting room for Manchester,

serving the packet boats that plied the river from May 1807 between Manchester and Runcorn. In 1821 the full trip lasted some eight hours in each direction, leaving the New Bailey at 8 am in summer and winter. The fares for such a trip were 3*s* 6*d* for the front cabin, and 2*s* 3*d* for the aft cabin.

Later years saw the introduction of through trips to Liverpool, which took seven hours, but neither this nor fare-reductions could prevent the trade being gradually taken away by the railways, and ending altogether in the 1860s.

The landing stage continued in use until the early years of the twentieth century for pleasure boat excursions, initially to the Pomona Gardens and later, after 1894, around the newly completed Manchester Docks.

In the entrance at the foot of the steps are displays and photographs about the landing stage and the man after whom the pub is named.

See also the Woden Street footbridge, also known as Mark Addy's Bridge, off Chester Road, a few yards above the head of the Manchester Ship Canal.

WHERE THE HYMN 'CHRISTIANS AWAKE' MAY HAVE BEEN WRITTEN

Access

On the western side of Littleton Road, via Whitewater Avenue.

Kersal Cell, Salford

This strangely named building, the earliest parts of which date from the late fourteenth century, has its origins in a legal grant made in 1142 by the Earl of Chester to the Cluniac priory of Lenton, near Nottingham. As a monastic establishment it was on a fairly small scale and probably had no more than two members at any one time.

The Cell was broken up at the time of the dissolution of the monasteries and the building passed into secular hands, being converted into a house.

Its chief claim to fame is that it was the home of the Jacobean hymn writer, poet and stenographer, John Byrom (after whom the city's Byrom Street is named). Local tradition has it that the hymn 'Christians Awake' was written in and first heard in the Cell in 1749, but it is more likely that Byrom was living in his Manchester town house at Hanging Ditch at the time.

The lower photograph shows the building in the early years of the twentieth century. It fell into a ruinous condition before the Second World War but was then rescued through the efforts of a preservation committee. In 1947 it was sold to become a country club and restaurant. By the early 1990s, when this photograph was taken, it was a club known as Byrom's and had had substantial extensions added to the rear.

In recent years the building has reverted to use as private housing, and the once-extensive grounds have been developed as a housing estate.

BUILT HERE TO AVOID SPOILING THE OWNER'S VIEW

Fletcher's Folly, Clifton Country Park

Access

Via Clifton House Road, which leads from Bolton Road (A666) to the country park.

This isolated chimney-stack is one of the surviving structures of the archaeologically significant Wet Earth Colliery site. The chimney was built in 1805 and was connected via large underground flues to a steam boiler at the colliery site some distance away. It was built here at the insistence of Ellis Fletcher, the owner of the colliery, who did not wish to spoil the view from his home, Clifton House.

The chimney had to be increased in height at a later date to serve an increasing number of boilers at the colliery, but the remote chimney arrangement was never very satisfactory and in the 1890s a replacement chimney was built at the colliery itself. The old chimney then became redundant, but instead of being removed completely was just reduced to its original height.

WHERE BRITAIN'S CANAL SYSTEM WAS BORN

Access

Off Worsley
Road, near
junction 13 on
the M60.

The Delph, Worsley

The Bridgewater Canal, Britain's first major artificial canal (though strong counterclaims are made for both the Sankey Brook Navigation at St Helens and the Exeter Ship Canal), was built between 1759 and 1765 by James Brindley for Francis Egerton, 3rd Duke of Bridgewater (the 'Canal Duke'). It was built to carry coal from the Duke's mines at Worsley to Manchester, and when opened it caused the price of coal in the city to drop dramatically.

Built at the same time, and equally remarkable, was this system of underground canals to reach the Duke's mines. The system, which eventually reached 52 miles in length, was built on four different levels and included an underground inclined plane. Special boats, known as 'starvationers', of differing sizes, were used in the system.

The two main entrances are located at Worsley Delph, and water issuing from the underground system carries the iron oxide deposits that for many years caused the water in the main canal in this area to appear the colour of tomato soup.

The right-hand side tunnel was first to be constructed, the second being added in 1771. Both tunnels met some 500yd inside the complex, and allowed a one way system to be used by boats, as shown in the engraving, thereby speeding up traffic considerably.

Use of the underground system ended in 1889, but access to parts was maintained by the National Coal Board up to 1968, when closure of Mosley Common Colliery made it unnecessary to maintain the system for drainage purposes. In recent decades subsidence of the tunnels has meant that such access is no longer possible. The distinctive colour of the canal's water will also soon be disappearing, as Salford Council has recently started to operate a filtration system to improve the water for local wildlife, although this change has not been without some local opposition.

A CANAL PASSENGER STATION

Packet Steps, Worsley

Access

Off Barton Road, close to the junction with the M60 and Worsley Road.

Located in front of the similarly named Packet House are these boat landing steps. Built in 1769, they were originally provided to serve the packet boat or passenger boat services that had run along the new canal to Manchester since 1766. The packet boats offered a smoother and safer ride than the stage coaches of the day, and refreshments were often served on board thereby avoiding the need to stop for this purpose.

In summer 1804 a packet boat trip left Worsley for Manchester at 7.30 am, arriving at 10 am, with a return trip at 4 pm. Another boat went in the afternoon and to Leigh every Monday.

In 1851 Queen Victoria and Prince Albert visited Worsley, travelling by canal from Patricroft on a specially built barge.

Victoria was impressed, writing later that 'the boat glided along in a most noiseless and dreamlike manner amidst the cheers of the people'. The cheers, however, frightened one of the two grey horses towing the Royal Barge, causing it to fall into the canal; the tow rope also broke, causing further delays.

As with passenger boats on the river navigations, the coming of the railways in the middle of the nineteenth century destroyed the canal packet boat business, but the steps remain in use today for the popular boat trips that operate along the canal on summer weekends.

See also, on the other side of the canal, the canal boathouse built for the Earl of Ellesmere's own barge.

WORSLEY'S INDUSTRIAL PAST

Fountain, Worsley Green

Access

As for the Packet Steps.

Many visitors to Worsley today have the idea that the attractive Green with its surrounding sought-after houses has always been like this. This is not so. The Green itself was up to 1903 the works yard of the Bridgewater undertaking, with its extensive mining interests and associated railways and canals.

When the yard was cleared the base of the old works chimney was retained and converted into this ornamental fountain, celebrating the achievements of the Canal Duke. A poem about the Duke written in Latin in 1905 is inscribed on the base.

THE CLOCK THAT STRIKES THIRTEEN TIMES

Access

On Worsley
Brow, at the
southern end of
Walkden Road.

St Mark's Church, Worsley

The clock in use at the church strikes thirteen times at 1 pm. This was initiated in the days when the clock was located in the Bridgewater works yard.

The Duke of Bridgewater used to spend time watching his employees at work in the yard. When he did this he noticed that they did not wish to leave their workplaces when the clock struck noon marking the start of their lunch hour. He also noted that when he stopped doing this they left promptly.

He became concerned when his employees started returning late from their lunch hour. Their 'excuse' was that they could hear the clock strike noon but they could not hear the single chime marking one o'clock when they should have been back at work.

The Duke was wise to this ruse, however, and with a wicked sense of humour arranged for the clock mechanism to strike thirteen times at 1 pm, or 'thirteen o'clock' as it has been described.

St Mark's Church itself was built in 1846 and was paid for by one of the Duke's successors. The clock was finally installed here in 1946.

ONCE A VIEWPOINT TOWARDS SIX COUNTIES

Ellesmere Memorial, Leigh Road, Worsley

Access

Located behind some houses on the northern side of Leigh Road (A 572), about half a mile west of Junction 13 on the M60. The best view is from the public footpath that runs north from the road.

This gaunt-looking and rather abandoned monument was originally some 132ft high. It was erected as a memorial to Lord Francis Egerton, 1st Earl of Ellesmere (one of the Canal Duke's successors), who died in 1857. The design was selected after a competition, which over 100 architects entered, the results of which were put on show at the Manchester Art Gallery.

The Earl was popular with his workers and tenants, and the £1,800 cost was all raised locally. Access to the top by stairs used to be possible, and it is said that on a clear day six counties could be seen. Admission was free to residents of Worsley, to others 1*d*, although in later years this increased to 2*d*, with free admission on Good Friday.

The structure was declared unsafe shortly before the start of the Second World War and Bridgewater Estates, the then owners, wanted to demolish it. After a local outcry a local man, who wished to remain anonymous, came forward with a donation to retain the top part. The central column was then removed and the top placed on the base, thus reducing the height of the tower.

Today it is not possible to get near the structure, and demolition was once more mooted a couple of decades ago. In early 2003 local papers announced that the Memorial was on the property market, with an asking price of £225,000.

A MEMORIAL TO A VERY PRODUCTIVE SOW

Polly's gravestone, Cock Hotel, Worsley

Access

On Walkden Road (A575), just south of its junction with the A580.

Located to the left of the hotel car park entrance is this unusual headstone, commemorating the death in 1904 of Polly, the mother of 200 pigs.

The Cock Hotel was built in 1930 and replaced an earlier inn that dated back to the seventeenth century, originally called the Meanley. That building stood just to the south of the present one and changed its name to the Cock Hotel early in the nineteenth century, when a stuffed game-cock stood in a glass case in the bar. Polly's headstone stands on the site of the old pub and, alas, is no longer her resting place.

Publicans of the past would often keep some livestock as a side venture, and some were farmers. Polly belonged to the publican, Mrs Alice Taylor, and was somewhat of a celebrity with visitors, who would come by wagonette to spend a day in Worsley and call at the inn for refreshment on the way home. As well as being a very productive mother, even by modern standards of agriculture, Polly had a great liking for beer. Visitors would be encouraged to subscribe to the cost of a gallon, which Polly obligingly would consume.

When the brewery were modernising the pub in the late 1980s there was concern that the little headstone would be swept away, and the local MP, Terry Lewis, made representations. Fortunately the brewery decided that it would keep and renovate the memorial to the feisty and fecund porker.

Luckily, someone had the good sense to take the photograph seen here of Polly when she was alive, showing her being fed her favourite drink probably by one of Mrs Taylor's sons.

In spite of local jokes, she did not give birth to all her offspring at the same time!

3

CURIOSITIES OF TRAFFORD

WHERE MANCHESTER'S BOTANICAL GARDENS ONCE STOOD

White City entrance, Old Trafford

Access

On Chester Road
(A56), close to
its junction with
Trafford Road.

This imposing structure is the sole surviving feature of the long defunct Manchester Botanical Gardens. The gateway, said to be similar to the original and opposite entrance gateway to the rural Trafford Park, was built when the Gardens opened in 1831, occupying a site of 16½ acres.

In 1857 the Gardens featured the Manchester Art Treasures Exhibition, opened by Prince Albert. In 1887, the year of Queen

Victoria's Golden Jubilee, the Gardens hosted the Exhibition of Arts, Science and Industry, which attracted a total of 4.7 million visitors.

The Gardens closed in 1907 and the site became Heathcote & Brown's White City Amusement Park. This lasted only a few years and in 1926 the site became a greyhound stadium, a use that continued until October 1981. The site and gateway then remained derelict for about ten years until developed as a retail park, during which the entrance gateway, which had survived all the changes of use of the site, was restored.

The two photographs show the gateway as it is now (opposite), and in the years when it was the entrance to the White City Amusement Park.

THE WORLD'S FIRST INDUSTRIAL ESTATE

Access

Just off the A56
at White City.

Trafford Park entrance mural, Trafford Road

The Trafford Park Industrial Estate, established in 1896 by Trafford Park Estates Ltd under the leadership of Marshall Stevens, was the first industrial estate in the world. Located next to the Ship Canal, it was established to gain benefit from and supply traffic to the then newly opened Manchester Ship Canal.

The estate grew rapidly, with many world-class large-scale engineering companies being established there. It made an outstanding contribution towards supplying Britain's requirements during the Second World War. At its peak over 70,000 people were employed within the estate.

After the war the estate underwent a long and gradual decline, which worsened in the late 1960s and '70s. To reverse this decline it was declared an Enterprise Zone in 1981, and from 1987 to 1998 was the subject of substantial public investment via the

Trafford Park Development Corporation, whose efforts led to a new road system, environmental schemes and other improvements to the estate.

At the main entrance to the estate from Manchester, the old Liverpool Warehousing building has been the location for two large murals by Walter Kershaw depicting industries in the Park. The first, dating from October 1982, was later replaced by the second, in November 1993.

The two photographs show both versions of the mural.

A Rural Survivor Within Trafford Park

Access

Off Trafford Park
Road. The
ecology park is
open only on
weekdays.

Trafford Park Lake/Ecology Park

Before being established as an industrial estate Trafford Park was the rural seat of the de Trafford family. In this setting the centre of the estate was Trafford Hall, now demolished. The estate also possessed a lake, dug in about 1860, with an area of about 8 acres.

The lake survived the establishment of the industrial estate and was used for boating and recreation up to the 1930s. Between then and the 1960s it was used as a tip, although it was never completely filled in as the steel works slag deposited there was periodically removed for use in construction projects.

Restoration of the old lake was first suggested in the 1970s but did not get under way until the 1980s, when the local authority and then the development corporation paid for its transformation into the Trafford Ecology Park.

The photographs show the lake in use in the early years of the twentieth century.

RAILWAY LINES THAT RAN ALONG THE EDGES OF STREETS

Access

The old railway lines may still be seen on Trafford Park Road, parts of Ashburton Road, and Mellors Road.

Estate Railway system, Trafford Park

When the industrial estate was first established transport links with both the adjacent Manchester Ship Canal and connecting railway systems were provided by the estate's freight railway system, which ran alongside the roadways of the estate past nearly every factory. At its peak the system extended to some 26 route miles and in 1940 handled some 2.5 million tons of goods.

After 1950, with the growing use of road transport, the estate railway system suffered a relentless decline, and was substantially cut back in scale in the 1970s. Despite some attempts at reviving the remaining system in the 1980s and 1990s use finally ceased in 1998, shortly after the Estates Company that had operated the system had been taken over by another concern.

THE CLOCK THAT ALWAYS SHOWS THE SAME DATE

Munich Clock, Manchester United Football Ground, Old Trafford

This clock bearing the date in 1958 when many 'Busby Babes' and officials of the football club died in the Munich air disaster is a reminder to the many thousands who pass it every match day. Twenty-three people died in the tragedy, including eight team members.

A plaque on the right-hand side of the East Stand records the names of those who lost their lives, and the excellent museum in the ground has appropriate displays and poignant mementos.

Manchester United Football Club has been at Old Trafford since 1910, and the ground is now one of the largest in the UK, capable of seating 67,000. The recently extended North Stand has the world's largest cantilevered roof.

One of United's own legends, Sir Bobby Charlton, has described the Old Trafford ground as being the 'Theatre of Dreams'.

Access

Located on the left-hand side of the East Stand, which faces Sir Matt Busby Way.

PLAGUE STONES, A BATTLE OF GIANTS AND A FORMER ENTRANCE GATEWAY TO TRAFFORD PARK

Gorse Hill Park entrance, Stretford

Access

Gorse Hill Park's main entrance is on the eastern side of Chester Road (A56), just south of Great Stone Road.

The origin of these stones, hewn out of a gritstone alien to the locality, has long puzzled local experts.

One story offered about how the stones came to Stretford concerns the mythical giant Tarquin, who lived in Knott Mill. He was a bad-tempered individual and one day got into an argument with another giant, from Stretford. During this he is said to have picked up a rock from out of the River Medlock and thrown it at the Stretford giant but missed.

Originally located on the western side of Chester Road they were later moved to the eastern side adjacent to the former Gorse Hill Farm and finally to their present location.

On top of the stones are two holes 7in deep. It is thought that these may have supported the shaft of a cross or two upright circular stones. During the Great Plague of 1665–6 the holes were filled with vinegar or holy water, in the mistaken belief that the spread of the disease could be halted if trading was done through putting money in the liquid. It is from this use that the stones gained their name.

The adjacent park entrance gateway was the former Chester Road entrance to the Trafford Park estate, and was originally located opposite the White City entrance gateway. This gateway was moved here in 1922.

ONE OF THE WONDERS OF THE WATERWAYS

Access

Barton Swing Aqueduct

This aqueduct carries the historic Bridgewater Canal over the Manchester Ship Canal. The Swing Aqueduct, first used on 21 August 1893, replaced James Brindley's 1761 masonry aqueduct which had carried the canal over the River Irwell.

The original idea was to lower the Bridgewater Canal down to the Ship Canal level on either side by means of boat lifts, but this was deemed too expensive.

Adjacent to the Barton Road bridge (B5211). The best view is from the south side of the Manchester Ship Canal.

The aqueduct was designed by Sir Edward Leader Williams, and is built in the form of a 235ft long iron trough which revolves around a central pier. In order to avoid delays on both waterways the trough is swung full of water. The latter, some 800 tons in weight, is kept in place by a system of metal gates which close both ends of the trough and the abutting ends of the Bridgewater Canal. To economise on space, the Bridgewater Canal towpath was carried across on a high platform inside the frame of the aqueduct, as seen in the lower photograph from 1936, although this has now been removed.

On the Salford side of the Ship Canal, on Barton Lane, can be seen part of one of the archways of the old Brindley aqueduct, built into the retaining wall at the side of the road in 1893.

TRANSPORT BY FERRY ACROSS THE SHIP CANAL

Access

Either via
Daresbury
Avenue,
Davyhulme, or
by the footpath
that leads from
the A57 near
Boysnope Wharf
on the approach
to Irlam from
Eccles.

Hulme's Bridge Ferry, Davyhulme

In these days of faster and ever more sophisticated means of transport, it is surprising to find this small passenger ferry still operating across the Manchester Ship Canal.

It was provided to replace an earlier footbridge, called the Hulmes or Holmes Bridge, that crossed the old Mersey & Irwell Navigation at this point. The building of the Ship Canal in the 1890s placed a legal obligation upon the Ship Canal Company to provide suitable alternatives for crossing the canal, and the obligation remains until the Company is excused by a fresh Act of Parliament.

This ferry, connecting Davyhulme with Boysnope Wharf, near Irlam, is still operated by the Canal Company, and uses a

rowing boat, which can carry a maximum of four passengers. The ferry is operated free of charge and has in recent years been provided with refurbished landing stages and an improved pedestrian access from the Davyhulme side.

Other ferries have operated across the Ship Canal within the area, but have now ceased operations. A small vehicular ferry ran from Irlam until the late 1960s, while Bob's Lane Ferry connected Partington and Cadishead until the early 1990s. The latter used a motor boat and from the late 1970s had been run with the support of the local Passenger Transport Executive.

A Relic of an Unfinished Country Estate

Brooks Drive, Hale & Timperley

This great tree-lined driveway, mainly unmade, is a reminder of the grand designs of the nineteenth-century banker, Samuel Brooks and his son, Sir William Cunliffe-Brooks. Samuel Brooks, who died in 1867, bought 800 acres in Hale and proceeded to develop it as a country estate. The central feature was to have been a great tree-lined driveway leading from what is now the Brooklands Metrolink station (named after the family) to Warburton Green.

Brooklands Road (today a main road) and the two stretches mentioned above were completed by father and then son, but the Warburton Green end was never undertaken and the 'estate' plan lapsed after Sir William's death. The estate was later broken up by sale in 1917.

A toll-house built by the Brooks still exists at the southern end of Brooklands Road, close to the roundabout.

Access

Brooks Drive runs in two lengths, both linked by Roaring Gate Lane. One stretch runs from the roundabout at the junction of Altrincham Road (A560) with Brooklands Road, while the other runs from Roaring Gate Farm to Hale Road (A538).

A Mysterious Defensive Mound

Watch Hill, Bowdon

Sometimes called Castle Hill, the origins of this Scheduled Ancient Monument are obscure. Located on the bank of the River Bollin at its confluence with a small tributary, and overlooking the A56, at this point a Roman alignment, it was clearly built for defensive purposes.

The earthwork, now overgrown with mature trees, comprises a gently sloping triangle of land formerly bounded by an outer ditch. At the apex of the triangle is a large circular mound surrounded by a well-defined ditch.

Excavations undertaken in the late 1970s failed to establish the date of its construction, but an early medieval date has been suggested.

The Only Toll-Bridge and -Road in Greater Manchester

Warburton Toll-Bridge

This toll-bridge is the only road crossing of the Manchester Ship Canal between the M60 at Barton and the M6 at Thelwall. It is also the only toll-bridge and -road within Greater Manchester.

It was built by the Ship Canal Company when the Ship Canal

was under construction, and replaced an earlier toll-bridge over the River Irwell which had been built in the 1840s to replace the old Hollins Green ferry. The old bridge still exists, forming part of the approach embankment on the Warburton side and the old toll-house stands next to the present tollbooth.

4

CURIOSITIES OF STOCKPORT

IS THIS THE UK'S LARGEST BRICK-BUILT ENGINEERING STRUCTURE?

Easily visible
from the A6 in
Stockport town
centre, or from
the bus station.

Stockport Viaduct

Dominating Stockport town centre, the railway viaduct has been claimed to be the largest brick-built engineering structure in the UK. Originally built for the Manchester and Birmingham Railway between March and December 1839, it first comprised some 400 cubic feet of stonework and around 11 million bricks. One writer in 1842 stated that the bricks used, if laid end to end, would exceed the whole length of the Great Wall of China.

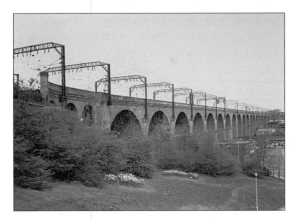

The viaduct was doubled in width in 1888–9. The total length is 1,780ft, with 26 arches, of which 22 have a span of 63ft each. The height of the parapet is 111ft above the River Mersey.

In the late 1980s the structure was cleaned and provided with floodlighting in a scheme carried out by British Rail and the local authority.

See also, in nearby Mersey Square, the Plaza Theatre and cinema, the only remaining 'super cinema' in Greater Manchester (although four other single screen venues also survive). Dating from 1932, the Plaza has recently re-opened, phoenix-like, after serving as a bingo hall since 1965. It is the venue for stage shows and twice-monthly vintage film nights, which feature performances on the theatre's original Compton cinema organ, complete with superb Art Deco illuminated surrounds.

AN UNUSUAL JEWELLERS

Winter's Clockhouse

Access

On Lower
Hillgate in
Stockport town
centre.

This shop was originally established as a jeweller's in 1859 and in about 1880 it was taken over by Jacob Winter. Prominent on the frontage are three painted figures (Father Time, a Victorian guardsman and a sailor), which struck the bells above every 15 minutes.

The left-hand shop window featured a unique hydraulically operated security device which lowered the entire window display into the shop cellar at the end of each day. Additional security was also offered by the fact that, like its neighbours, the shop was built into a sandstone rockface and has no rear exit.

The shop closed down because of declining trade in 1988 and the clock was later damaged by a passing vehicle, but in 1991–2 it was restored and reopened as a wine bar and restaurant, called appropriately Winter's, and its clock mechanism can be seen in working order by patrons.

NAMED AFTER ITS STAIRCASE

Former Staircase Café, Market Place

Access

On Market
Place.

This rather incongruous-looking building, at the time of writing being photographed behind hoardings and scaffolding, is another of Stockport's most historic buildings, and has been the subject of considerable local effort to secure its preservation.

The shop itself is built around a fifteenth-century cruck frame, while the cellar shows signs of medieval origin. Rising from the rear of the building, for its full height, is an intricately carved early seventeenth-century staircase, which gave the former café its name. The staircase is said to be of a rare type for the North-West, and is described as a caged newell staircase, in which the four inner newell posts rise the full height of the building without interruption.

Many of the upper floor rooms have seventeenth- and eighteenth-century oak panelling of high quality suggesting that the building

was of some local significance, such as the town house of a notable county family.

Unfortunately, fires in November 1989 and the mid-1990s damaged some seventeenth-century areas at the rear of the property, and parts of the roof. In the mid-1990s the property was bought by the local authority and a bid, ultimately successful, was made for National Lottery funding for a full restoration scheme. Work on this is now under way and the building has been re-roofed. The scheme is being carried out in conjunction with developments on adjoining sites, and will provide a new tourist information centre and a site for the Stockport Story display currently located in the Vernon Park Museum. It is scheduled to be completed by Easter 2005.

See also the Heritage Centre in the nearby Stockport Parish Church. The church was the first location for Stockport Grammar School, the second oldest school with a secular foundation in the UK.

STOCKPORT'S MOST HISTORIC HOUSE

Great Underbank Hall

Access

On Great Underbank, in the town centre.

This building is said to be Stockport's most historic house. Its exact age is unknown but it is thought to date from the late fifteenth or early sixteenth centuries.

It was the town house of one of Stockport's most influential families, the Ardernes of Bredbury, who owned it until 1823, when it was sold at auction. At the time of the sale attempts were made to turn the building into a town hall for Stockport, but it was bought by a syndicate comprising W. Miller Christie, Isaac Lloyd, John Worsley and J.K. Winterbottom, who formed the Stockport and Cheshire Bank.

It was first used as a bank in 1829, and became one of the first branches of the District Bank Ltd, which itself became part of the NatWest Group in 1968.

The front of the hall contains original oak panelled rooms, with 'eight-light' windows that run almost continuously along the lower storey. The rear is a large banking hall, built in 1915, containing a magnificent seventeenth-century fireplace. Over the fireplace is a plaque commemorating the initial founders of the bank, and a list of the branch managers from 1829 to the present day. The branch manager's office also contains a similar fireplace.

The whole building remains in use as a bank and is sympathetically maintained by NatWest.

The remains of Arden Hall, the home of the Ardernes, can still be seen on Castle Hill, just off Ashton Road in Bredbury.

THE 'CHESTERGATE HILTON'

Air Raid Shelters, Chestergate

Access

Opening times
vary.

Stockport's extensive air raid shelter system was excavated in the soft sandstone by the local authority in the months following the Munich crisis of September 1938, and was one of the few large shelter systems to be provided outside London. Three separate systems were excavated, at Brinksway, at Dodge Hill and Chestergate on the south side of the town centre. The latter was the largest and was built as extensions to existing shallow caves.

The shelters were equipped with electricity, wooden seating, steel beds (many of which remain *in situ* today), toilets (both water and chemical) and a First Aid post. They saw extensive use during the Second World War, being referred to locally at one time as

the 'Chestergate Hilton', but towards the end of the war they were closed up and largely forgotten.

During the 1980s ideas began to emerge about opening the Chestergate site up for tourism, and in 1990 Stockport Museum began running guided tours through them. Part of the system has since been re-equipped as it would have been during the war, and visitors can now wander round these areas. Guided 'Explorer' tours (with miners' helmets and lamps) are also available in the undeveloped rear parts, which have been left as they were at the end of the war as, so the guidebook says, 'a dark and forbidding reminder of the suffering caused by war, as well as a tribute to the ingenuity and will to survive of an earlier generation'.

DESCENDED FROM THE HEIGHTS OF MOUNT TABOR

Access

In the small seating area at the junction of Edwards Street and Wellington Road South.

Column capitals, Wellington Road South

The four detailed stone capitals located in this small paved garden and rest area are all that remains of the former Mount Tabor Methodist Chapel, a substantial building which stood on this site.

The Chapel was built when members of the earlier Mount Tabor Chapel in Middle Hillgate, part of the Methodist 'New Connexion' branch, outgrew their premises. Constructed between October 1865 and May 1869 at a cost of over £9,000, the new building could seat 900 worshippers. The main entrance at the front was up a massive flight of steps that extended across the front of the building. This supported a lofty portico consisting of four columns topped by these Corinthian capitals, hewn from Darley Dale stone.

Underneath the building were rooms used by the chapel's Sunday school, which at its height had 38 teachers for its 278 boys and girls. During the Second World War the Sunday school rooms were used as the local food rationing office, and later as temporary offices of the local authority's housing department.

The chapel was demolished in 1969 but had not been used for religious purposes for some years since the remaining congregation had joined the Trinity Methodist Church.

Opposite is Stockport Town Hall, with its distinctive 'wedding cake' architecture. When the building was being erected it was not possible to include bells within the main clock tower, as it was feared that these would disturb patients at the former Stockport Infirmary, on the other side of the A6. The Town Hall also contains some interesting original toilets provided for the use of members of the Council.

For a notable church that is still standing see St Thomas's on Higher Hillgate. Built in 1825, it is Greek revival in design and is fronted by six massive Ionic columns.

A ROMAN SIGNAL STATION?

Peel Moat, Heaton Moor

Access

Adjacent to the
footpath across
Heaton Moor
Golf Club, which
leads from
behind the Peel
Moat Recreation
Centre,
Buckingham
Road, to
Barcicroft Road,
Burnage. Peel
Moat itself is on
land belonging
to the golf club,
which does not
welcome
trespassers.

This curious earthwork is a perfect square, its sides facing due north, south, east and west. It comprises a slightly raised central mound with sides 110ft long, surrounded by a moat the outer sides of which are 220ft long.

The origins of Peel Moat have puzzled local historians. The name itself suggests a defensive purpose, and it may have been put to such a use. Other proposals include an association with local hunting, a protected site for animals, or a Roman survey marker.

The most convincing explanation comes from Stockport Local History Librarian David Reid, who suggests that it was a Roman signal station associated with the fort at Castlefield.

A COLD WAR SURVIVOR IN CHEADLE

Regional War Room, Cheadle

Access

This is difficult, as it is hidden away behind the Alexandra Hospital on Mill Lane, and visitors should not attempt to cross the hospital site. The war room can be best seen from passing trains on the Stockport to Altrincham railway line.

This ugly concrete-and-brick structure, completed in 1952 as a Government Regional War Room, was designed to withstand the blast of a Hiroshima-sized atomic bomb. It was built around a two-storey map room, the lower storey being underground. Accommodation was provided for about fifty staff, and the complex had its own generator, water system and protected communications links.

The concept of the war room was largely rendered redundant by the advent of the H-bomb in the later 1950s, and its function as a Regional War Room ceased in 1958, when it was relegated to a sub-centre of a Regional Seat of Government.

In 1964 the complex was taken over by Manchester Corporation and used by the Civil Defence Corps until its disbandment in 1968. Subsequently the centre was kept on a 'care and maintenance' basis until 1981, when it was reactivated as the Greater Manchester Council's main emergency control centre and some internal alterations were undertaken. This status ceased in 1991 following which the centre lay unused while its owners, by then the Greater Manchester County Fire & Civil Defence Authority, decided what to do with it.

It has recently been sold to the Alexandra Hospital which intends to demolish it to provide more car parking for the hospital site, and so it may disappear completely in the near future.

A MILL BUILDING TOPPED WITH FRUIT

Access

Adjacent to
Stockport Road
(A560), on the
north bank of
the River Goyt,
below Vernon
Park.

Pear New Mill, Bredbury

Built in 1912, this mill building was to be the first phase of a larger project but the second phase, to be called Apple Mill, was not built.

The mill comprises a five-storey main structure built in red Accrington brick with yellow brick and terracotta decoration, with a two-storey carding extension on the west side. A separate engine-house has Art Nouveau terracotta panels.

The most distinctive feature of the mill is the pear-shaped dome of the water tower at the south-east corner of the building, but

there are also two smaller pear-shaped decorations at the western corners of the main roof.

The mill ceased to be used for textile purposes in 1966 and it is now the Pear Industrial Estate. The main pear feature has recently been provided with floodlighting.

MARPLE'S MEMORIAL TO SAMUEL OLDKNOW

Headstone from Mellor Mill, Marple

Access

Located in the Memorial Park, in the centre of Marple.

This circular headstone is situated close to the old Marple stocks and an old sundial which came from the long-demolished Marple Hall. The headstone bears Samuel Oldknow's initials and the date 1790 when construction work on Mellor Mill was started.

Samuel Oldknow was born in Anderton, Lancashire, and it was there in the early 1780s that he commenced as a muslin manufacturer. In the following years his enterprises grew rapidly and he acquired factories in Stockport and the surrounding areas. In 1787 he purchased the Bottoms Hall Estate between Marple and Mellor, and on it he built Mellor Mill, arguably his crowning achievement.

Oldknow was also involved in the Peak Forest Canal as its principal promoter, improvements to local roads, coal mining and the building of the Marple lime kilns. After 1793 his businesses were beset by financial problems and many were sold off or leased out. Oldknow died in 1828 but his mill remained in production until 1892, when it was destroyed by fire.

Some of the ingenious water systems for supplying the mill with water power can still be traced around the mill site, and the mill ponds (or 'lodges') were developed after 1892 as the Roman Lakes for recreational purposes, in which use they remain today.

A BRIDGE DESIGNED FOR THE CONVENIENCE OF CANAL HORSES

Roving Bridge, Canal Junction, Marple

Access

At the top of Lockside, which runs up the canal from Posset Bridge.

The canal locks and junction at Marple are a popular destination for Sunday afternoon walks, and are the location for several curiosities relating to the canals. At the canal junction itself is this graceful 'roving bridge', built in the days when canal narrow boats were pulled by horses.

The bridge is designed to allow a northbound horse pulling a boat from the Macclesfield Canal to cross the canal from the towpath on the eastern side of the canal on to the Peak Forest Canal (which was on the western side), without the boatmen having to unhitch the towing line from the horse as it crossed the bridge. The same advantage applied of course in the reverse direction.

See also the old 'stop lock', designed to prevent one canal company getting 'free' water from its neighbour, on the south side of the bridge, and the old toll office on the bridge itself.

TUNNELS FOR BOATMEN AND HORSES

Posset Bridge, Marple

Part way down the flight of locks is the curiously named Posset Bridge, built by Samuel Oldknow in 1894. The name is said to have been based on the fact that he allowed his workforce a 'posset' of ale from his public house, the Navigation Inn, which formerly adjoined the canal.

The bridge itself has two small tunnels, one to gain access to the adjacent lock, and the other (shown here) to take the canal towpath under the roadway.

Access

Where the Marple to New Mills road (B6101) crosses the canal.

See also, a short way down the canal from here, the attractive warehouse complete with boat-loading hole that Oldknow built to serve Mellor Mill.

RELICS FROM MARPLE'S INDUSTRIAL PAST

Access

Via Lime Kiln
Lane, off the
B6101.

The Lime Kilns, Marple

Associated with the Peak Forest Canal are the Marple Lime Kilns. These formerly occupied a large area bounded by the canal and the Marple–New Mills road, and had their own canal branch from Posset Bridge. They were finished in 1797 and were another product of Samuel Oldknow.

It is said that Oldknow built the lime kilns to provide work for the husbands of the women he employed at Mellor Mill. Although the lime kilns were not profitable for Oldknow they continued in use until the early years of the twentieth century, and were even lived in at various times.

The front wall of the kilns occupied a very visible site, and was therefore provided with windows with Gothic-style tracery to improve the façade's appearance, although this was offset by the kiln's six chimneys. The kilns comprised four large tunnels running into the canal bank. The limestone itself was fed into the top of the kilns at canal level and the burnt lime was then removed to dispatching buildings, which survive nearby as housing.

The pleasantly landscaped remains we see today are only a limited reminder of the area's industrial past. They give little indication of the former gothic façade of the kilns themselves, as shown on the photograph opposite, taken after work done in the mid-1970s which involved bricking up the tunnels and hiding some of the masonry.

A Relic from Compstall's Industrial Past

Access

Within the country park, close to the weir.

Derelict coal barge, Etherow Country Park, Compstall

This old coal barge lying derelict in the mud is a reminder of Compstall's industrial past.

Compstall Mill and its adjacent village were developed by the Andrew family after 1820, and in some respects Compstall was

a model industrial village run by a benevolent owner. A large mill reservoir or 'lodge' was dug to serve the mill's water wheels, and was supplied with water from the River Goyt via a navigable canal or mill leat that led from the still-impressive weir about a mile up the valley.

This leat, not connected to the rest of the canal system, was used to transport coal mined from small pits up the valley, at a time when steam power was used to supplement the original water power. The tub boats of which these remains are an example were made of riveted cast-iron plates. Approximately 22ft long, 16ft 5in wide and 3ft deep, they could carry about 8 tons of coal. They would have been drawn by horses, which would have pulled several barges in each trip.

The mill ceased to be used for textile purposes in 1966 but the use of the navigation had ceased much earlier, possibly at the time when the mill was fully converted to electricity in 1915. It is said that the boat was first placed here in the 1920s.

Many years ago proposals were made to rescue this barge and renovate it but it still remains here, quietly rusting away.

See also, further up the valley, the remains of the inclined tramways used for transporting the coal to the leat, and the abutments of the former bridge which carried the tramway over the river.

A MONASTIC PRESENCE IN ROMILEY?

Chadkirk Chapel, Romiley

This small chapel, somewhat hidden away in a pleasant location in the Chadkirk Country Estate, owes its origins, it is said, to a religious oratory established on the site by St Chad, Bishop of Lichfield AD 669–72.

There are mentions of a chapel here in 1347, and by the sixteenth century it had the status of a 'Chantry chapel', where masses for the dead were said.

At the time of the dissolution of the monasteries it was claimed as a family chapel by the Davenports of Henbury, near Macclesfield, but this claim was disputed and the chapel was seized by the Crown. Later it was restored to the Davenports, following which it fell out of use.

Access

Close vehicular access is discouraged owing to the location in the Country Estate. Parking is available just off Otterspool Road (B6108). Then follow either the well-signposted trail, or the road through the park towards Romiley.

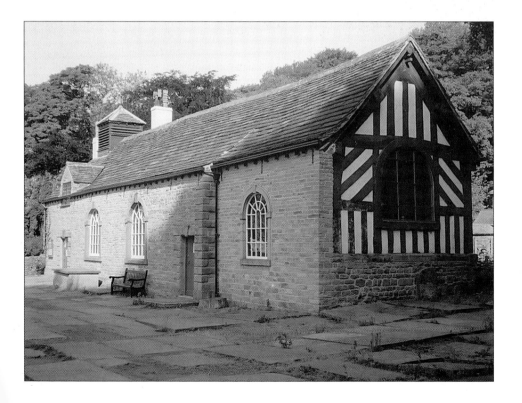

By the 1640s it was being used by Puritan dissenters, and in 1689 it was formally registered as a nonconformist place of worship. The nonconformists were evicted in 1705, and again a period of disuse followed.

After falling into a ruinous condition it was restored by public subscription in 1747, from which date it served as Romiley's parish church until 1866. It was restored again in 1761, in 1860 and 1876. In 1971, after being used only for occasional Sunday afternoon services for some time, it was declared redundant and sold to the local authority when the adjoining Country Estate was being first developed. Further restoration followed in 1973, and again in 1994–5. It is now open to the public on a regular basis at weekends.

The earliest part of the building dates from Elizabethan times, but other sections are Georgian. The bell is inscribed '1750 God be with us all'.

5

CURIOSITIES OF TAMESIDE

THE LARGEST MORAVIAN SETTLEMENT IN THE UK

Access

Off Fairfield
Road, which is a
continuation of
Market Street.

Fairfield Moravian Settlement, Droylsden

This settlement is the largest of its type in the UK (although Fulneck near Leeds comes a close second) and is an outstanding Conservation Area, with all of its buildings 'listed' as being of architectural or historic interest.

The Moravian Church is the oldest 'free church' in northern Europe, pre-dating the Reformation by some sixty years. It was founded in 1457 out of the work of the Bohemian martyr John Hus.

Fairfield was founded in 1784, after the congregation had been obliged to move from Dukinfield where their landlord had refused to renew their lease. The church building was finished in 1785,

and boys' and girls' schools started in 1790 and 1796 respectively. The overall design was the responsibility of the leader of the Settlement at the time, the Revd Benjamin La Trobe (1728–86), whose second son, Benjamin Henry La Trobe (1761–1820), was involved with both the White House and Capitol Buildings in Washington DC.

'Community Houses' were provided for single brothers and sisters, and the graveyard is unusual in that there are no standing headstones, the single sexes are separated and no grave is ever reopened.

The urbanisation of the surrounding area caused pressure on the self-contained community, and nonbelievers were allowed to reside in the Settlement from the 1850s. The Boys' School closed in 1896 and the Girls' School was transferred to the local authority in 1919. The Theological College closed in 1958.

Despite these changes the Settlement, with its cobbled streets and Georgian houses, remains an oasis of peace and quiet. The old Theological College was restored a few years ago, and guided tours of the Settlement are available.

A GARDEN VILLAGE IN TAMESIDE

Broadway Garden Village, Droylsden

Access

Either off Ashton Hill Lane, or via Fairfield Road off the A635.

This small estate, immediately adjacent to the Moravian Settlement, comprises thirty-nine houses built between 1913 and 1922. Designed by the Manchester architects Edgar Wood and James Henry Sellars, it was built for a cooperative housing venture, the Fairfield Tenants Association Ltd, a group of Moravians who wished to be near the Settlement. There is a variety of houses, detached, semi-detached and terraced, all built in a refined Georgian style.

One of the initiators, Hedley Smith, described the aims of the schemes as 'to make Droylsden a better place to live in . . . in addition to providing gardens for each house, it was hoped in a new housing scheme to provide a bowling green for the use for the tenants. Rich people had gardens on three sides of their houses and there was no reason why working classes should not have theirs.'

The original scheme was to have been much larger, but lack of money led to the remaining land being sold off to private builders for development.

A LAKE CAUSED BY A LANDSLIP

Crime Lake, Daisy Nook

Access

At the junction of Cutler Hill Road, Ashton Road and Stannybrook Road.

Crime Lake was formed in 1799 when a culvert provided for a stream under the newly opened Hollinwood Branch of the Ashton-under-Lyne Canal was blocked by a landslip. The resulting collection of water behind the canal embankment eventually reached the level of the canal itself and in subsequent years the canal bank between the two disappeared.

The Daisy Nook area, being a relatively rural pocket surrounded by industrial Oldham, Ashton and Manchester, has always been a popular venue with nearby townsfolk and today's country park is well used. Boating on the lake was popular in the nineteenth century, and was tried again a few years ago. A funfair has operated for many years at certain bank holidays, and the scene was painted by L.S. Lowry.

In 1854 the lake water froze for a period of thirteen weeks, and stalls were set up on the ice to serve the visiting public.

Until 1855 the area was called Waterhouses but the name Daisy Nook was adopted after the name appeared in a short sketch written by the dialect poet, Ben Brierley, about a holiday taken at Daisy Nook on the day the news of the fall of Sevastopol reached Manchester.

Daisy Nook contains one of only two areas of land owned by the National Trust within Greater Manchester.

REMAINS OF INDUSTRIAL ACTIVITY AT PARK BRIDGE

Access

Either down the old railway incline from Alt Hill Road, or by the footpath which leads from Mill Brow. The site is provided with helpful information boards.

Rocher New Pit, Park Bridge

Looking rather like the remains of a Cornish tin mine, although sadly defaced by graffiti, is this surviving stone structure from the Rocher New Pit, sometimes called the Nelsons (India) Pit. Coal mining in this locality is said to have started in the 1650s. The pit head gear incorporated a waterwheel, fed by a leat from the nearby River Medlock. The leat still contains water and can be seen close by.

At a later date steam power was used for pumping purposes, and in 1791 the Birmingham firm of Boulton & Watt supplied to the then owners, Barrow Lees & Co, a 6–7-stroke engine capable of lifting water 107yd. Some pits in the area were far deeper.

Mining finally ceased here in about 1886, when the mine was under the control of the Rocher Colliery Co. Ltd.

The Park Bridge area is full of reminders about its industrial past, centred on the steelworks controlled by the Lees family. The works is said to have supplied the rivets used in making the Eiffel Tower. There is an interesting visitor centre in the old stables building, and recently the site of the Fairbottom Bobs pit engine (which was transported to his Dearborn, Michigan museum by Henry Ford in 1929) has been excavated.

BUILT TO CELEBRATE THE MARRIAGE OF THE PRINCE OF WALES

Hartshead Pike, Ashton-under-Lyne

Hartshead Pike dominates the north east of Ashton. Located 943ft above sea level, it commands fine views of the east of Greater Manchester (and it is said four counties), and is a popular, if windy, venue for a Sunday afternoon visit.

Originally a beacon site, the present structure is said to be the third on the site since 1426. The Pike was rebuilt between 1751 and 1758 but in 1794 the structure was split open by lighting. It developed a huge crack and eventually fell down in 1820.

Access

Either a short energetic uphill walk from the end of Lily Lanes, off Lees New Road, or for lesser mortals, via Brookbottom Road, Mossley.

The final rebuilding was undertaken by John Eaton in 1863 in commemoration of the marriage of the Prince of Wales (the future Edward VII) and Princess Alexandra. It was originally to have been 85ft high but in the end was capped off with a conical roof when either money or commitment to the project ran out.

It was cleaned in 1977 to celebrate the Silver Jubilee of Her Majesty Queen Elizabeth II, and has recently received floodlighting.

A RELIC FROM THE DAYS OF CHARTIST UNREST

Access

On the northerly
side of Mossley
Road (A670)
about three
quarters of a
mile from Ashton
town centre.

Entrance gateway to Ladysmith Barracks, Ashton

This entrance gateway and surrounding perimeter wall, complete with gun embrasures, are the sole surviving structures from Ladysmith Barracks.

Construction of the Barracks started in 1841 and was a response by the government of the day to threatened industrial unrest in the area, Ashton being at the time a centre of the Chartist movement. Finished in 1845, the Barracks were home to various cavalry and infantry regiments until the Manchester Regiment was formed in 1881. The Regiment was based here until 1958 until it amalgamated with the Kings Regiment and moved to Warrington, the Barracks being finally vacated at this time.

After 1958 most of the buildings, apart from the Army Pay Office, were demolished and the site remained vacant until used for the Roland Bardsley housing development in 1988.

WHERE THE MOST FAMOUS MILITARY SONG WAS WRITTEN

Judges, Corporation Street, Stalybridge

Access

In the centre of Stalybridge.

The plaque on this building is close to where the most famous military song of the First World War, 'It's a Long Way to Tipperary', was written.

The song was written by Jack Judge (1872–1938), a music hall entertainer and composer of popular songs. Born in Oldbury in the Black Country, Judge was performing at the Grand Theatre in Stalybridge in January 1912. One night, after the evening's performance, he went to a club and was teased about a song he had performed that night. As he was leaving the club he was challenged to write a new song the next day and perform it on stage that evening. The bet was for 5 shillings.

On the way to his lodgings he overheard a fragment of conversation containing the words 'It's a long way to . . .', and promptly seized upon this as his song title, adding the name 'Tipperary', although some sources say that the original place was

Connemara. Judge had never been to Ireland, although he had grandparents from County Tipperary.

The following day he went to a pub opposite the theatre, the New Market Inn, and composed the song, the music being taken down by Horace Vernon, the theatre's musical director. Needless to say, Judge won his bet, and first performed the song on 31 January 1912.

Later, in recognition of financial help given earlier, he allowed his friend Harry Williams to be credited as joint author, and they shared the royalties.

With its catchy tune the song became famous when popularised on the music hall circuit, but its real fame came when it was adopted by the 7th Battalion of the Connaught Rangers Regiment, who were heard singing it in 1914.

The New Market Inn, located to the left of the Conservative Club, ceased to be a pub in 1932 and became the Stalybridge Celtic Supporters Club. The plaque was placed on the building in 1953, being unveiled by bandleader Jack Hylton. The building had become derelict by 1980 and was demolished, when the plaque was transferred to the building then housing the Stalybridge Old Band Club. This has now become a bar, called appropriately 'Judges'.

THE LONGEST AND SHORTEST PUBLIC HOUSE NAMES IN BRITAIN

The 13th Cheshire Rifleman Inn, Stalybridge

Access

Approximately half a mile north of the town centre, on Astley Street.

This public house rejoices in the full name 'The Old Thirteenth Cheshire Astley Volunteer Rifleman Corps Inn', which is said to be the longest public house name in Britain.

The pub dates from 1855 when it was a beerhouse called the New Inn. By 1880 the 13th Cheshire Rifle Volunteer Corps drill hall was nearby, and by 1902 its name had become The 13th Mounted Cheshire Rifleman Inn. In 1956 the beerhouse became a full public house, and the first edition of the *Guinness Book of Records* confirmed that the name was the longest pub name in the UK.

The 1966 edition of the book mentioned that the word 'Mounted' was often omitted, but failed to mention an alternative contender for the title. The twentieth edition in 1973 confirmed that another pub elsewhere was in first place, but the title was reinstated by the time the 27th edition came out in 1980. First place was lost again a few years later, but was reinstated in 1987, when the brewery added three new words to the title, giving it 55 letters in total.

Despite this, the name is often shortened to The 13th Cheshire Rifleman Inn.

The Q Inn, Market Street, Stalybridge

Access

On Market Street, adjacent to the railway bridge.

On Market Street, in the centre of Stalybridge, is the Q Inn, said to be the shortest public house name in Britain. This name is a comparatively recent innovation by the brewery, but for many years there was indeed a Q Inn on the former Back Grosvenor Street. This started life in 1842 as a beerhouse, known as the White House. Two years later it had become a full pub, and by 1848 was being referred to as the Q Inn, although it was sometimes called the Queens Hotel. It ceased being a public house sometime before 1935, and the building has long since gone.

While in Stalybridge, another licensed hostelry worth visiting is the Buffet at Stalybridge station.

CARRBROOK'S MYSTERIOUS CASTLE

Buckton Castle, Carrbrook

This small earthwork, a scheduled Ancient Monument, was once thought to date from the Iron Age, being either a druidical temple or some form of solar observatory. Recent excavations suggest that the site dates from before 1066, was being used until the twelfth or thirteenth centuries, and was built by either the Earl of Chester or the Lord of Longdendale. It was noted on a local survey as being ruined by 1360.

The site is 1,123ft above sea level and comprises a raised oval platform surrounded by a steep bank and on all but the south west side by a ditch up to 15ft deep. The central platform, about 100ft long and 75ft deep, is artificially raised above the surrounding ground level. Archaeologically, it is known as a 'ringwork'. There is said to be some evidence of stonework having been part of the original structure.

It has been rumoured that gold is buried on the site, and evidence of excavations undertaken in 1730 to find this is still visible.

The site was used as a beacon during late medieval times, one such occasion being to mark the defeat of the Armada in 1588.

Access

Not accessible to the public, as it lies on the edge of an active quarry. It is best seen from a distance on Castle Lane, near Castle Farm.

DENTON'S TH'OWD PEG

Access

On Stockport
Road (A6017) to
the south of
Denton, close to
Town Lane.

St Lawrence's Church

This distinctive wooden church, built in 1530–1 as a Chapel of Ease through the aid of two local landowners, the Hyde family and Sir Richard Holland, is known locally as Th'Owd Peg on account of the fact that originally no nails or metal were used in its construction, only wooden pegs. Externally, the black and white decoration is painted over plaster, timber and brick infilling.

It was substantially repaired between 1816 and 1839, and after becoming the local parish church in 1854 it was completely restored between 1859 and 1862, when the old box pews and original pulpit were removed. In 1872 it was considerably remodelled by M. & H. Taylor and extended: two transepts and a chancel were added in the same style to create a cruciform plan. At the same time the west gallery and a belfry were added.

The church was known as St James's Church until the early nineteenth century, when the curate of the day, the Revd William Parr Greswell, decided to change the name, it is said, on account of the fact that the Denton Wakes holiday (which then comprised only one day) fell on St Lawrence's day.

See also in the churchyard the two-stepped mounting block, provided to help the less active and wealthier churchgoers to mount their horses after attending church.

A CRUCK-FRAMED BUILDING

Newton Hall, Hyde

Built in 1370, this cruck-framed building is one of the earliest surviving structures of its type in the UK.

The method of construction is such that the blades of each cruck beam start on a ground sill and extend up to support the roof timbers. The windows are typical of the fourteenth century, and were closed internally by shutters known as 'window doors'.

Prior to its restoration the building had been preserved by being encased in brick, with a roof of blue slates. The building does not appear to have been black and white originally as would have been normal for this type and age of building.

The Hall was restored between 1968 and 1970 by its enlightened owners, the adjoining Sir William Kenyon & Co. During restoration the oak beams were fixed as originally with hand-made pegs fastening the joints. About 1,200 of these were used, and about 35 per cent of the timbers in the building are original.

A glass panel, extending the whole height of the building, allows visitors to see exactly how a medieval timber-framed hall was constructed.

Access

On Dukinfield Road. The building is not normally open to the public, but close inspection from the grounds is possible.

REMINDERS OF EARLIER CORONATIONS

Access

In Market Place,
on the road
leading from
Mottram to
Broadbottom.

Crown Pole, Mottram

Standing in front of the old Courthouse, this metal pole, complete with weathervane, street lighting and direction signs, dates from 1926. It replaced a wooden pole originally provided in 1760 to commemorate the coronation of George III.

The village stocks in front of the Pole were placed here after being unearthed during the building of the nearby Hattersley overspill estate during the 1960s.

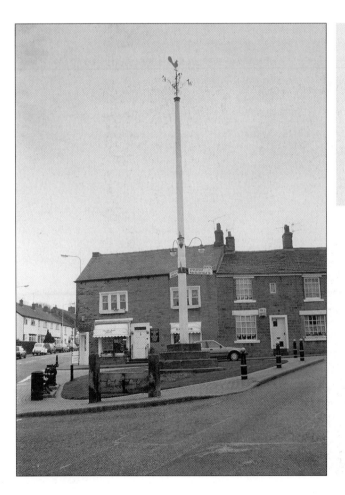

See also the elaborate drinking fountain, in front of the old Courthouse, built to mark the provision of a public water supply to the area in 1888. Many similar fountains, mostly now inoperative, abound in the county.

WHEN THE MOTTRAM WATCHERS PREVENTED BODY-SNATCHING

Black Bull's Head datestone, Mottram

Part way up the stone steps that link Church Brow to Mottram Church is this doorway, still with its 1769 datestone, of the old Black Bull's Head Inn, which closed in 1911.

Access

Off Church Brow, which leads northwards off Market Place.

In the early part of the nineteenth century the inn was frequented by a local vigilante group known as the Mottram Watchers, whose aim was to prevent body-snatching from the exposed and relatively isolated churchyard nearby.

In the churchyard itself, close to the north-east corner of the church, one of the gravestones (for Lewis Brierley, a boy who died in 1827) contains this reference to the body snatchers:

> To wretches who pursue this barbarous trade
> Your carcasses may in turn be conveyed
> Like his, to some unfeeling surgeon's room,
> Nor can they justly meet a better doom.

The hill on which the church is placed, known as Warhill, is claimed to be the site of an important battle between the armies of King Stephen and Queen Matilda, the daughter of King Henry I, in the twelfth century. There is no documentary evidence to substantiate this story, but the quarrel was ended by the Treaty of Wallingford whereby Stephen was allowed to keep the throne on condition that Matilda's son (crowned as Henry II) succeeded him, which happened in 1154.

The parish church is worth visiting (open some Saturdays). It contains many interesting features including stone effigies of Sir Ralph and Elizabeth Staveleigh, wooden bread racks dating from 1619 and 1737, which were used for placing loaves baked specially for distribution to the poor of the parish, and an altar rail carved by Robert Thompson (the 'Mouseman of Kilburn') containing his usual 'signature' – a tiny carved mouse placed in some inconspicuous corner of the work.

THE LAST HOME OF A GREAT ARTIST

The Elms, Mottram

Access

On Stalybridge Road, close to the village centre.

This rather gaunt house was the last home of the great artist L.S. Lowry, who lived here from August 1948 until his death in 1976.

Lowry, who had previously lived in Salford, was enticed to buy the house via an architect friend. He is said to have remarked that one of his requirements for a place to live was that it should be close to a railway station. Despite this, the nearest railway station (at Broadbottom) was nearly 2 miles away.

Lowry let it be known that he detested Mottram, although he was granted freedom of the borough in 1956 by the Longdendale Urban District Council. He lived what has been described as an ascetic life in the place, barely maintaining the house and keeping it, as some have described, at sub-zero temperatures. A telephone was only installed in 1968 after a burglary but even then Lowry did not take incoming calls. He never travelled outside the UK.

On the other hand he was generous with genuine admirers and helped many young artists further their careers. He acquired a great number of paintings, particularly by Rossetti, and after his death these had to be cleared from the house along with a large number of his own works. His artistic legacy has been given its proper recognition in the new Lowry Centre in Salford.

Since 1976 the property has been brought up to date in its external appearance, and is now privately owned.

AN ENTOMBED AMPHIBIAN IN MOTTRAM?

The Frog Stone, Mottram

Access

This is difficult to find as it is fairly small. It is above head height in the retaining wall on the eastern side of the A6018 leading to Stalybridge, close to the Roe Cross Inn.

This peculiar stone was originally split by the navvies engaged in building the turnpike road in 1825–6. At the time the cutting, known locally as Mottram or Deep Cutting, had taken up to twelve years to complete. Its retaining wall was one of the highest ever built as a drystone wall (i.e. without mortar pointing), although in more recent times it has been pointed.

The navvies called it the Frog Stone because a frog is reputed to have jumped out when the stone was split. Inside the hollow was a perfect impression of the frog, and the local populace arranged for the rest of the hollowed out stone to be painted white, thereby highlighting the impression. This painting is still visible today, though now somewhat worn.

Stories of frogs and other amphibians jumping out of rocks and coal were quite commonplace in the nineteenth century, and in the 1860s there were letters to *The Times* about it. A Frenchman is also said to have buried a number of frogs in mud and to have found some of them alive twelve years later.

A simpler explanation of the name for the stone is that the hollow in a brick for holding the cement is called a 'frog'.

A STONE ASSOCIATED WITH A CAPED CRUSADER

The White Stone, Roe Cross, Mottram

Access

Located within a private curtilage just off the Old Road near the Roe Cross Inn.

This white boulder, repainted at intervals, is associated with the legendary Sir Ralph de Staveleigh of Stayley Hall, sometimes called 'Sir Ro', after whom the area Roe Cross is named. Before going to fight in the Crusades Sir Ralph is said to have cut his wedding ring in two with a single slash of his sword. Both he and his wife then pledged fidelity towards each other by keeping their respective halves of the ring.

While away he was taken prisoner by the Saracens. One night he had a dream that some evil was about to overtake his wife, causing him to wake, fall to his knees and pray to the Almighty. He then fell asleep again, and awoke to find himself in England on the road to Stayley Hall at the spot now marked by the White Stone.

In his absence it had been assumed he had died in the conflict, and his 'widow' was claimed by another knight, whose intentions were clearly her wealth, lands and property.

On the wedding day the assembled crowds were joined by a caped stranger, actually Sir Ralph. At the appropriate moment he threw off his cape in time for his wife to recognise him and place their halves of the ring together. The impostor then fled.

A similar story, with a slightly less agreeable ending, is connected with Mab's Cross in Wigan. Unfortunately, in Sir Ro's case the story is out by about 200 years, as he lived from about 1377 to 1419, well after the Crusades.

A SYMBOL OF THE RESURRECTION IN MOSSLEY

Access

St George's
Church is on
Stamford Street,
the main road
leading from
Ashton-under-
Lyne. Access to
the interior of
the church is
normally only
possible when
church services
are being held.

Kenworthy Memorial, St George's Church, Mossley

This strange memorial is to be found at the rear of the church. It shows a young girl dressed in a funeral shroud lifting her coffin lid. Some suggest that the memorial represents Christ's Resurrection.

The memorial actually commemorates the death, on 23 February 1776, of Catherine Kenworthy, aged 18, the only daughter of local benefactors Cornelius and Dorothy Kenworthy.

It was first placed in the original Mossley Church, which was built in the eighteenth century, but was transferred to the present building, which was completed in 1882.

6

CURIOSITIES OF OLDHAM

A CELEBRATION OF OLDHAM'S JUBILEE OF 1899

Access

Via the King's
Road entrance to
the park.

Observatory, Alexandra Park

The parks and recreation grounds of urban Greater Manchester still contain examples of buildings, monuments and curiosities erected in Victorian times when many of the parks were first laid out. These are often now dilapidated or vandalised and suffering from lack of maintenance, although a few are beginning to be restored with Millennium or Heritage Lottery money, and such a scheme is currently being carried out at Alexandra Park.

This pagoda-like structure will serve as an example of the more unusual feature. It was built in 1899 to commemorate the Jubilee of Oldham's incorporation as a Borough, its foundation stone being laid by the Mayor, Councillor Jackson Brierley, on 15 June 1899.

Access to the top has not been possible for many years.

A MEMORIAL TO OLDHAM'S BELLMAN

Old Blind Joe, Alexandra Park

Access

Close to the Observatory.

This stone statue commemorates Joseph Howarth, who was town Bellman from 1820 to 1860. The post of Bellman was similar to that of Town Crier.

The statue was presented to the Parks Committee in 1863, a year after Old Joe's death. Old Joe was born blind but had a phenomenal memory, and it is said that he was able to recite word perfect a whole chapter of the Bible after hearing it read only once.

He was also a noted lay preacher. Oldham's noted historian, the late Hartley Bateson, indicates that the statue was erected to honour Old Joe's services to religion, not his post of bellman.

FAILSWORTH'S CORONATION REMINDER

Failsworth Pole

Looking rather like a war memorial, the present brick-built structure of Failsworth Pole was built in 1953 to celebrate the Coronation. It is 54ft high and contains a gilt-painted 'Cock of the North' on its top.

It is at least the fifth pole to stand on this site, where the village maypole was probably erected during the Middle Ages. The first 'political' pole was erected on 1 January 1793 'to the

King, Church and the present Glorious Constitution'. It blew down through decay in October 1819.

The second pole, a ship's mainmast 78ft high, was erected on 24 August 1850, and the third pole, costing over £100, some 92ft high and topped with a solid copper cockerel, dated from 24 August 1889.

The fourth pole was erected on 24 August 1923, was 82ft high and imported from Louisiana. It cost £300, which was raised by public subscription, but it too was destroyed in a gale, on Easter Monday, 10 April 1950.

FUNERAL ARRANGEMENTS OF THE PAST

Hearse House, Saddleworth

Access

On Church Lane, opposite Saddleworth parish church.

In times past many country areas had the use of what was effectively a 'village hearse' for use in times of bereavement, particularly for the paupers of the parish. It was usually a long black cart, complete with lid, and sometimes decorated with black plumes at each corner. A local farmer would usually supply a horse to pull it.

The hearse would be kept in a building close to the local church, as here, provided by the parish authorities. A stone plaque above the doors contains the date 1824, the names of the two churchwardens (James Taylor and George Ogden), and the inscription 'Know Thyself' in both Greek and English.

Similar buildings exist close to Hyde, Marple, Mellor and Mottram parish churches. They usually fell out of use in the later nineteenth century, when firms of undertakers became commonplace.

See also, outside the church, the old village stocks dated 1689, and an old horse and carriage mounting platform.

A NATURAL FEATURE USED AS A WINE HOLDER FOR GROUSE SHOOTERS

Pots and Pans Stone, Greenfield

Access

Via Kinders Lane
and Boarshurst
Lane. Then
approximately a
thirty-minute
walk up a steep
and stony path –
for serious
walkers only!

This distinctive stone, formed out of Millstone Grit, is located high above Greenfield, and, together with the adjacent War Memorial built in 1923, is visible from miles around.

It was at one time thought to have been a druidical sacrificial altar. On its top side are smooth holes, caused by weathering. It is rumoured that early in the last century these were deepened to hold the wine, supplied in pots and pans, to gentlemen grouse shooters.

MEMORIAL TO A ROYAL VISIT AND AN UNSOLVED MURDER

Yeoman Hey and Bills-o-Jacks Plantations, Greenfield

The stone in the foreground, built into the wavewall of the Yeoman Hey Reservoir, commemorates a visit to the site by the King of Tonga in 1981. In the background are the Yeoman Hey and the Bills-o-Jacks plantations.

The latter plantation is associated with the macabre Bills-o-Jacks murders that occurred in 1832. These took place in the Moorcock Inn when the landlord, William Bradbury, and his son Thomas were bludgeoned to death in circumstances which were never explained. Interest in the crime at the time was high, an estimated 30,000 sightseers visiting the site out of morbid curiosity on the following Sunday, and 10,000 attending the funeral.

The Moorcock Inn itself was demolished at about the time the Yeoman Hey Reservoir was built in 1880.

Access

Either via the car park at Dovestone Reservoir, or the Binn Green car park, off the A635. Then a healthy walk in each case.

THE LONGEST CANAL TUNNEL IN THE UK

The westerly entrance to the tunnel is located a few yards from the Diggle Fields car park on Sam Road, opposite to Clydesdale Road.

Standedge Canal Tunnel, Diggle

Standedge Tunnel, part of the Huddersfield Narrow Canal, is the longest canal tunnel in the UK and the highest point on the connected canal system.

Work on the tunnel first started in 1795 but was not completed until 1811, at a cost of some £160,000. It was slightly extended at the Diggle end in 1893–4 when alterations were being made to the adjoining railway alignments. Its total length is now 5,698yd, and it took the old boatmen some three and a half hours to 'leg' their way through the tunnel.

The Huddersfield Narrow Canal was the last of the three trans-Pennine waterways to be completed, and was the least successful. Even for a canal the speed of traffic was very slow because of the large numbers of locks climbing the distances on either side of the tunnel, and the different gauges of connecting canals obliged transhipment between boats at Huddersfield. Traffic had evaporated by the early years of the twentieth century and the canal was officially closed in 1944.

The canal has recently been restored and reopened following work carried out since the 1970s, and traffic can once more use the tunnel, although boats are obliged to utilise a compulsory towage system in which they are pulled by a battery-powered boat.

More information about the canal and tunnel can be found at the canal visitor centre at the Marsden (Yorkshire) end of the tunnel (admission payable), from where short-distance boat trips run into the tunnel at summer weekends.

THE LAST GAS STREET LAMP IN GREATER MANCHESTER

Gas Lamp, Delph

Access

Adjacent to the
main street, in
the centre of the
village.

In times past street lighting in towns and cities was provided by gas lamps, and in many areas this remained long after the widespread introduction of electricity. It was the replacement of (coal-produced) town gas by natural (North Sea) gas in the late 1960s that finally saw the end of gas street lighting in the UK.

The picturesque village of Delph, historically part of Yorkshire's West Riding, was the last place in Greater Manchester to have gas street lighting, which lasted until the mid-1970s.

Here a token reminder has been retained in working order.

A Memento of the Turnpike Era

Milepost, A62, Delph

Apart from toll-houses, another feature that survives from the turnpike era of road building is the milepost or milestone. Made of metal or stone, these survive in some of the rural fringes of the county where the turnpike trusts were most active.

As well as assisting direction, their purpose was to aid both the road trust and the traveller to calculate the distance travelled and therefore the toll payable.

This is a well-preserved example, first erected by the Wakefield and Austerlands Road, Upper Division.

Access

On the northerly side of the A62, close to the former Delph station.

WHEN THE ROMANS RULED BRITAIN

Access

Off the A63
above New
Delph, and
overlooking
Castleshaw
Reservoir.

Castleshaw Roman Fort

There are in fact two Roman forts at Castleshaw. The first was an auxiliary fort built in AD 79–80 at the same time as the adjacent road was built linking Manchester (Castlefield) to Chester and York, during the period when Julius Agricola decided to conquer the north of England. It was approximately one day's march from Manchester.

This fort had earth ramparts approximately 9ft high and extended to about 2½ acres in area housing about 480 auxiliaries. It was in use for only about ten to fifteen years.

The second fort was established at the start of the second century AD, when a smaller fortlet was constructed inside the ruins of the earlier fort. This only had a small garrison and served mainly as an administrative, industrial and storage facility. It remained in use for only about twenty years, and is one of the smallest in the UK.

Further details on the construction and use of both forts are available on the two excellent information boards provided at the site.

7

CURIOSITIES OF ROCHDALE

A CHURCH WITH A WOODEN TOWER AND THE OLDEST WAR MEMORIAL IN THE UK

St Leonard's Church, Middleton

Access

On St Leonard's Street, just north of the town centre, overlooking Jubilee Park.

This church, a Grade I listed building, dates predominantly from 1524, but the tower and porch date from 1412 and there are traces of the original Norman church also remaining.

It has one of the three remaining wooden church towers in existence in Britain, locally described as a 'wooden steeple for a

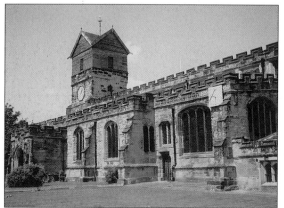

stubborn people', which was built on top of the tower in about 1709 in order to allow the church bells to be hung a storey higher. It has been suggested that wood was used because the sandy foundations of the tower would not bear additional weight, also that the wooden structure would allow a sweeter tone of the bells to be heard.

An interesting feature is the stained glass window dedicated to the Middleton Archers who fought at the battle of Flodden Field in 1513 that is thought to be the oldest war memorial in the UK. It was provided by Lord Richard Assheton, who at the age of 32 had led his archers, whose names may be seen on the window.

The church originally had six bells, later increased to eight. These regularly rang the 'curfew' at 9.50 pm from 1819 until 1939, and on special occasions since.

See also the Boar's Head Inn, opposite the town's library. This is said to be of twelfth-century origins, and is owned by the local authority. It is rumoured that a secret tunnel runs between the pub and the parish church but no evidence of this has yet been traced.

THE WIDEST BRIDGE IN THE WORLD

The Esplanade, Rochdale

Access

In the centre of the town, close to the Town Hall.

Rochdale was listed until recently in the *Guinness Book of Records* as having the widest bridge in the world, with a total width of 1,460ft. The blue plaque placed on it, however, only claims that it is the widest bridge in Europe.

The bridge, now a ferro-concrete structure across the River Roch fronting Rochdale Town Hall, and forming a large part of the Esplanade, originated in the early seventeenth century. It was first extended from Yorkshire Street to Wellington Bridge in 1904, but was successively made wider in 1910, 1923 and 1926.

The adjoining Rochdale Town Hall was built between 1866 and 1871 and designed by W.H. Crossland of Leeds. It is renowned for its stained glass, carvings and ceramics, and contains a large mural of the Magna Carta. The building is 303ft long and the tower 190ft tall. The original tower was some 50ft taller, but its spire was built of wood and was destroyed by fire in 1883.

The building is reputed to have impressed Adolf Hitler in the days before the Second World War, who saw it as a superb example of British architecture. It is claimed that in the event of Britain being defeated by Germany, Hitler had plans to transport the building stone by stone to a new site in Germany.

See also, in the churchyard of the parish church (up the steps behind the Town Hall), the gravestone of John Collier, the Lancashire dialect poet known as 'Tim Bobbin', who died in 1786.

THE BIRTHPLACE OF THE CO-OPERATIVE MOVEMENT

Toad Lane Museum

Widely accepted as the birthplace of the first successful co-operative society, formed by twenty-eight workers to sell good food at reasonable prices, this shop first opened on the evening of 21 December 1844.

Co-operative societies in the North-West had been tried before the Toad Lane enterprise but all had gone to the wall either through being run on too idealistic lines, or by being unable to survive in times of distress.

The initial stock of the shop comprised only 28lb of butter, 56lb of sugar, 2cwt of flour, a sack of oatmeal and some tallow candles. The shop only opened two nights a week initially, but soon was opening every night except Tuesdays. The payment of a dividend to members and the guarantee of pure food ensured the success of the movement.

The building is owned by the Co-operative Union, which has operated it as a museum since 1931, the reconstruction being partly funded with cash from the Japanese, who are noted supporters of the movement. The displays inside give an insight into the ideals and the principles of the Co-operative movement.

In front of the building is this combined post-box and street lamp, and nearby is a stone memorial to the victims of the Kobe (Japan) earthquake of 16 January 1995.

'Th' Wayvers' Sayport'

Hollingworth Lake

The centrepiece of its own country park since 1976, Hollingworth Lake was one of many reservoirs built to supply water to the Rochdale Canal, being completed in 1804. Since 1923 its waters have been used for drinking water supply.

The lake became a centre for day-trippers in mid-Victorian times when the Rochdale Canal Company granted rights over the lake to James Sladen and Henry Newell. It was particularly popular at Whitsuntide (after the locals had been on their 'Whit Walks'), and an Easter Fair was held at the spot known as Lakebank. For many years it was referred to as 'Th' Wayvers' Sayport'. Even today, though it has only a rudimentary beach, with its amusement arcades, catering establishments and the occasional bed and breakfast guest house, it still has a slight air of the traditional 'seaside'.

HOLLINGWORTH LAKE.

Paddle steamers were introduced in 1856, and the proprietors of the hotels and public houses that catered for the day-trippers also provided rowing boats, a skating rink, a dance floor and steam horses (known as 'Bobby Horses').

Captain Webb is said to have trained on its waters for his famous cross-Channel swim and also took part in competitions. In 1881 he competed and won against J.A. Jennings, watched by a crowd of 2,000.

The lake was also used for ice skating when it froze over completely in 1860 and 1864, when 2,000 skated. In 1874 a horse and cart were driven across the frozen lake, although in that same year three people drowned when the ice broke. On another occasion a cricket match was reputedly played on the ice. It froze again in 1902, 1912, 1947 and 1963.

High above the lake can be seen the M62 Trans-Pennine Motorway, with the graceful Rakewood Viaduct, the only one on the motorway originally lit by floodlighting.

A Reminder of Buildings Flooded by a Reservoir

Access

Turn north off
the A58 between
Rochdale and
Littleborough,
and proceed
through Wardle
village to the end
of the road.

Wall of History, Watergrove Reservoir

Watergrove Reservoir was built by Rochdale Corporation to provide for the growing water needs of Rochdale. It holds some 720 million gallons of water when full, and was built partly as an unemployment relief project. Work first started on the scheme in August 1930 and was finished in 1938, the official opening ceremonies being performed on 6 April.

The waters of the reservoir drowned a large valley, containing the village of Watergrove, farms, houses and the Watergrove and Roads mills. Other buildings standing in the catchment grounds of the reservoir were also demolished.

This Wall of History, incorporated into the wavewall at the reservoir, contains many of the namestones and datestones of the houses, farms and mills that had to be demolished when the reservoir was built.

Greater Manchester's 'Roman' Road

Roman road, Blackstone Edge

Access

Off the A58 about a mile east of Littleborough.

This ancient track, thought by many to be a Roman road – although this claim has been strongly disputed – is clearly one of the historic routes linking Lancashire and Yorkshire. The road is surprisingly well preserved in places and is sturdily constructed with a cambered surface of large cobbled stones. Overall it is 18ft wide, with a central channel of larger troughed stones down the middle that appears to serve no useful purpose.

Its straight alignment over the crest of the hill and the occasional find of Roman coins at one or two nearby locations supports the view that it is of Roman origin, connecting Manchester to Ilkley, where there was an important Roman fort. The alternative view is that the road is a medieval packhorse route. At its Yorkshire end it is referred to on some maps as Dhoul's Pavement.

It was certainly used by Daniel Defoe in August 1705, and he noted in his diary that he got lost in a blizzard on the way.

The road was replaced on an easier alignment by a turnpike road in 1735, and by the current road in 1786. It is crossed by the Pennine Way close to the Yorkshire boundary.

Access

Close to the summit of Blackstone Edge, where the 'Roman' road crosses the Pennine Way.

A MEDIEVAL WAYSIDE MARKER

Aiggin Stone, Blackstone Edge

This distinctive stone is believed to be a medieval wayside cross, at least 600 years old. It is carved with initials and a cross. A plaque nearby notes that it is now under the care of a local society in Littleborough.

8

CURIOSITIES OF BURY

THE PUB WHERE THE 'TOASTED CHEESE CLUB' USED TO MEET

Access

At the junction
of Market Place
and The Wylde.

The Two Tubs public house

This public house is believed to be the oldest building in Bury, dating from the early eighteenth century. It was constructed around two existing oak trees (since removed).

The name of the pub dates from the 1830s and is said to have been decided upon when a competing hostelry decided to erect a new sign. Regulars of the pub, particularly members of a group called the Toasted Cheese Club, decided that their watering hole, then called the Globe, could not be outdone.

Someone suggested that two barrel halves be fixed above the door (to represent the two hemispheres of the world) and so the name came about, although the Globe continued to be used as the pub's official name until the 1990s, when it was finally supplanted by the Two Tubs.

Since this photo was taken the pub has received a makeover, and the two barrel halves are now placed on the gable wall of the building.

See also Bury's famous black pudding stall in the central market.

THE CLOCK TOWER WHERE EVERY STONE WAS NUMBERED

Whitehead Clock Tower

Access

At the junction of Manchester Road and Knowsley Street, to the south of the Town Hall.

This tower was built in 1914 through the benefaction of Henry Whitehead, in memory of his brother Walter Whitehead, a local doctor with a wide reputation who had been a surgeon and an ex-President of the British Medical Association. It was built on the site of a mansion called Belle Vue that had been demolished some years earlier.

The structure is built of Portland stone and is 57ft high. Built by F.M. & H. Nuttall, it is said to be of late-Tudor design and has a canopied sculpture representing 'Time' on its front.

The tower was one of the last works of the architectural practice of Maxwell and Tuke, who were also responsible for Blackpool Tower, and who had offices in both Manchester and Bury. It is reported that every stone for the tower came to the site ready numbered to be placed in position.

A MEMORIAL TO THE INVENTOR OF THE FLYING SHUTTLE

Access

On Market
Street.

John Kay Memorial, Kay Gardens

This monument is another gift of Henry Whitehead to the good citizens of Bury. It commemorates John Kay, who was born in nearby Ramsbottom in 1703 and invented the flying shuttle in 1733, which revolutionised the weaving industry.

The monument, designed by a Mr Gough of Bristol, takes the form of a domed pavilion with four statues depicting weaving, mining, agriculture and engineering, together with bronze panels of textile machinery and a list of Kay's other inventions, such as improved methods of spinning twine and mohair, and wind- and horse-powered pumps.

WHERE DICKENS'S 'CHEERYBLE BROTHERS' FIRST SAW THEIR ADOPTED TOWN

Grants Tower, Ramsbottom

Access

Via public footpaths uphill from the A56, a few hundred yards north of the Red Hall Hotel and restaurant. It is close to a modern mobile telephone mast.

In 1783 brothers William and Daniel Grant came to Ramsbottom after escaping the crop failures in Scotland. They were seeking new lives and livelihoods and soon found both, with remarkable success, after they had acquired a calico print works established by Sir Robert Peel, whose son founded the Metropolitan Police.

The Grants helped Ramsbottom turn from a small agricultural community into a thriving township. They were in some respects model employers, and made efforts to end the infamous 'truck' system by which workers were paid partly with tokens for use in company shops instead of cash. They personified all the positive aspects of the Victorian era and were immortalised by Charles Dickens as Ned and Charles Cheeryble in the novel *Nicholas Nickleby*.

They also bought land and provided important local buildings, including Nuttall Hall Farm, sadly now demolished, built in the Scottish baronial style complete with a feature tower.

In 1828 they built Grants Tower, on the exact spot where they are reputed to have paused before deciding to make Ramsbottom their home. Located on a hill called Top o' th' Hoof, it was dedicated to the memory of their parents. The 80ft high tower built of locally quarried millstone grit became a focal point for visitors.

In the early days of the Second World War the tower was used as a Home Guard observation post, but owing to neglect over the years it fell down in 1944 and has been a ruin ever since.

A BRAND-NEW VICTORIAN RAILWAY STATION

Access

On Railway Street, close to its junction with Bridge Street.

Railway station, Ramsbottom

Looking every bit as though it has stood here for decades, this solid-looking Victorian station is a completely new building, only opened to the public in 1989.

The railway line from Bury to Rawtenstall stopped carrying passengers in 1972, and freight in 1980, but through the efforts of the East Lancashire Railway Company the whole line has been re-opened in stages since July 1987 and operates on most weekends, usually with steam-hauled trains.

The new station is said to have been designed with some of the features of the original station, which was built in 1846 and demolished in 1971. The adjoining level crossing, whose signal box dates from 1939, is said to be one of the few in the country still to be manually operated.

Further evidence of the Grant brothers' influence on Ramsbottom is easy to find. Apart from the Grant Arms Hotel, they also built St Andrew's Church in 1834, originally consecrated as a Scottish Presbyterian church. This was re-consecrated for the Church of England in 1875, after the brothers' successor, nephew William Grant, himself a High Anglican, had ejected the Presbyterians in 1869. The 29ft pendulum from the church clock is reputed to be the longest in the country.

THE MAN WHO REPEALED THE CORN LAWS AND FOUNDED THE METROPOLITAN POLICE

Peel Tower, Holcombe Brook

This tower was built to commemorate Sir Robert Peel, founder of the Metropolitan Police and Prime Minister from 1841 to 1846, who was born near Bury in 1788. The 128ft high tower was erected in 1851 following his death the previous year. It is 1,162ft above sea level and visible for miles around. The tower cost £10,000, all the money being raised locally by a committee, who in true northern fashion wanted the building to be topped with battlements. Above the entrance is a simple, single inscription – PEEL – in bold relief. In the base is an extract from his resignation speech.

A combination of vandalism and weather meant that internal access to the tower was blocked off for many years, but visitors have been able to climb to the top again since the late 1980s. A Union Flag is normally flown from the top when the tower is open.

Access

A visitors' car park is available off Lumb Carr Road (B6214) which leads from Holcombe Brook to Haslingden. There is then a steep climb to the Tower.

A statue of Peel is located in Market Place in the centre of Bury. It shows a sheaf of wheat at his feet, in recognition of his repeal of the Corn Laws in 1846.

GREATER MANCHESTER'S ONLY VILLAGE LOCK-UP

Access

On Harwood Road, next to the junction with Turton Road.

Tottington Dungeon

Rural areas such as the Peak District contain frequent examples of the village lock-up, but examples in urban areas are few. The Tottington Dungeon built in 1834 is the only surviving example of such a structure within Greater Manchester. It was built at the rear of the former public house at the road junction (not to be confused with the present Old Dungeon Inn, which is a few doors away up the main road), and probably replaced an earlier less secure structure on the site.

It was originally looked after by the publican and would normally have been used to allow drunkards and other miscreants

the opportunity to 'cool down' overnight; less commonly it may have been used for the temporary imprisonment of offenders awaiting trial in the local towns. Its predecessor is said to have had links with the highwaymen who operated in the nearby Affetside area.

In 1840 it was taken over by the local bobby, and until 1964 the keys and handcuffs belonging to Mr Wilkinson, the one-time Tottington Parish Constable, could be seen hanging in the Old Dungeon Inn. The handcuffs can now be seen in Bury Museum. The dungeon was probably taken out of use in 1884, when Tottington was provided with a police station equipped with two cells.

Some decades ago one of the Salford museums proposed moving the dungeon stone by stone to a new site but this idea was dropped after a local outcry. It is currently owned by the local authority. No one appears to have any explanation of the meaning of the various crude carvings with which it is embellished.

A Tower Built to Keep Up With the Neighbouring Mill-Owners

Tower Court, Tottington

Access

Off the road linking Greenmount and Tottington, via Shepherd Street.

This 60ft-high neo-Norman castellated tower was built in the 1840s by the Tottington industrialist Joshua Knowle. Its original purpose was to stable the heavy cart horses used for transport at his nearby calico print works (long since demolished).

It is said that in the early nineteenth century Knowle had regarded Nuttall Hall Farm, built by the Grant brothers in neighbouring Ramsbottom, as a wonderful manifestation of their success. He had been one of their managers at the time, and when he was in a position to do so he decided to build an almost exact replica.

After the closure of Knowle's mill the tower was incorporated into a farm called Tower Farm, which was converted in the early 1990s into a mews-cottage-type development called Tower Court.

AN ANCIENT MONUMENT IN RADCLIFFE

Access

On the eastern
side of Radcliffe,
via Sandford
Street, which is
off the A6053.

Radcliffe Tower

This ruined tower, a scheduled ancient monument since the 1920s, lies close to the historic St Mary's Church. It is not known when precisely it was built, but it is thought to have been erected by local landowner James Radcliffe in 1403, although some think it is even older.

The tower was originally connected to a substantial, timber-framed Great Hall, and was built for defensive purposes, being close to a bend in the River Irwell.

By the early nineteenth century both tower and hall were in a dilapidated condition and being used as a hayloft and cowshed. The hall was demolished in about 1840 but the tower continued to be used for agricultural purposes until the 1950s, and its site was excavated in 1964. In the 1980s the tower's surroundings were tidied up by the company that operated the nearby tip.

Local opinion on the tower has been summed up by one writer thus: 'We're proud of it, but what do we do with it?'

9

CURIOSITIES OF BOLTON

A REMINDER FROM THE DAYS WHEN BOLTON WAS A MILL TOWN

Access

Close to the
Town Hall and
Deansgate.

Mill Engine, Oxford Street

This mill engine, now encased in glass and rotating in slow motion with the use of electricity, was made in Bolton by Hick Hargreaves & Co. Ltd, and is said to be similar to many steam engines made in the town.

Until 1969 it operated at a mill in Bentham, Yorkshire; it was placed on display at this location in the early 1970s.

The county has several other interesting steam engines that can be seen by visitors. The steam winding engine used at the former Astley Green Colliery, now the Red Rose Steam Centre (open Sundays), has the largest colliery winding engine used in the Lancashire coalfield. Trencherfield Mill, in Wigan, has the world's largest working mill engine, while the engine at the Ellenroad Engine House, Milnrow, is claimed to be the largest and most complete spinning mill steam engine surviving.

WHERE TO FIND KEY EVENTS IN BOLTON'S HISTORY

Churchgate Cross

This cross is said to be similar to one that stood on the same site from 1436 to 1786, which itself replaced an earlier structure dating from the thirteenth century. Such a cross would mark the effective centre of towns – usually the marketplace.

In August 1748 John Wesley was stoned by a crowd as he stood on the steps of the cross. He wrote:

> At one I went to the cross in Bolton. There was a vast number of people, but many of them were utterly wild. As soon as I began speaking, they began thrusting to and fro; endeavouring to throw me down from the steps on which I stood. They did so once or twice, but I went up again and continued my discourse. They then began to throw stones; at the same time some got upon the cross, behind me, to push me down. . . .

The present structure was presented to Bolton on 29 November 1909 by George Harwood, one-time Member of Parliament for the town. Plaques around the lower part list key events in Bolton's history over a 700-year period ending in 1909.

Access

At the Churchgate/ Deansgate/ Bradshawgate junction in the town centre.

A REMARKABLE SURVIVOR

Steam crane, Manchester, Bolton and Bury Canal

Access

From Ladyshore
Road – car park
at the eastern
end, then a 5–10
minute walk
eastwards along
the canal
towpath.

This derelict steam crane, located on the towpath of the Bury branch of the canal, was at one time used to lift coal-carrying containers from barges to the yard of the former Mount Sion Bleach Works, the buildings of which are located on adjacent low-lying land. The crane was erected in 1875, and was made by J. Smith & Sons of Rodley, Leeds.

The crane's survival is surprising since it must have been out of use for over fifty years, the canal at this location last being used to transport coal from Ladyshore colliery in 1949.

Proposals have been made recently by British Waterways for an ambitious scheme to restore the Manchester, Bolton and Bury Canal to navigation and to re-connect it to the main canal system by 2006.

A CHURCH TOWER WITH NO CHURCH

Ringley Tower

Access

On Fold Road, which is just off the Kearsley to Whitefield Road (A667).

This church tower, close to Ringley Bridge (a scheduled ancient monument), is all that remains of the second church at Ringley, built in 1826 to a design by Charles Barry, who later designed the Houses of Parliament.

The church was demolished in 1859 and was replaced by the present church. At the same time the old tower was repaired and raised in height by several feet. A clock was installed in 1907.

A stone in the wall of the tower commemorates the building of the first chapel at Ringley by Nathan Wallwork in 1625.

Other isolated church towers, often remaining after demolition of the adjoining churches, can be seen in other parts of Greater Manchester, examples being located at Salford, Heaton Norris and Marple.

The old village stocks, dating probably from the seventeenth century, are on the opposite side of the road. The village of Ringley was the setting for a local Wakes week tradition known as the Mock Mayor of Ringley, which took place on the first Monday in May. The Mock Mayor was not an official position but the holder was entitled to have a free pint of beer and other items from each of seven local public houses that were passed on his 'procession'. He was obliged to dress in his best Sunday clothes, and read out a 'proclamation' – usually a list of sports and games that were to take place that day. At the end of the proceedings the Mayor was thrown from the bridge into the Manchester Bolton and Bury Canal. The tradition died out before the Second World War, but was revived on a couple of occasions in the early 1990s.

AN UNUSUAL SIGNPOST

Signpost, Bradshaw

Access

At the junction
of Bolton Road
and Bradshaw
Road (A676).

This signpost, together with the inscription, is built into the corner property at the road junction. Erected in 1838, it points the way to Bolton, Bury, Edenfield, Haslingden and Burnley.

On the opposite side of the road, standing on its own, is all that is left of the old Chapel of Ease of Bradshaw. It remained standing when its adjacent church was replaced by the new building close by in 1872. The old tower was restored through local efforts in 1985–6, and was re-dedicated on 18 September 1986.

THE BIRTHPLACE OF SAMUEL CROMPTON

Firwood Fold

Access

Off the eastern side of Crompton Way (A58), close to the junction with Tonge Moor Road.

This delightful settlement has been a Conservation Area since 1967, and has been subject to improvement schemes in the past couple of decades. Its chief claim to fame is that it was the birthplace of Samuel Crompton, inventor of the spinning mule, who was born to George and Betty Crompton in the house with the thatched roof (3 Firwood Fold) on 3 December 1753.

The Crompton family moved to the nearby Hall i' th' Wood in 1758, and it was there in 1779, after five years' development work, that Samuel completed his famous invention, a spinning wheel able to spin yarn to a stronger standard but still fine enough to be used in muslin production. This innovation, which combined the moving carriage of the spinning jenny with the water rollers of the water frame, revolutionised the local textile industry and laid the foundations for its nineteenth-century prosperity.

A Reminder of Past Religious Troubles

Access

Via Smithills
Dean Road, off
Crompton Way.
Opening times
of the Hall vary.

Bloody footprint, Smithills Hall

This footprint, preserved in stone, is alleged to be that of the Revd George Marsh of Deane. In 1554, during the reign of the Catholic Mary Tudor, Marsh – a Protestant – was asked to swear allegiance by local magistrate Robert Barton, owner of Smithills Hall.

Shortly after leaving the room in which the hearing took place Marsh is said to have stamped his foot in the passageway, proclaiming that if his faith were true a mark would remain for all time. He was subsequently imprisoned in Lancaster and Chester, where he was burnt alive in 1555.

Ghostly occurrences are said to have resulted in the Hall when the stone was once removed, and even today it is rumoured to become wet with fresh blood each year on the date of his death.

ONCE KNOWN AS THE DESERTED VILLAGE

Barrow Bridge

This picturesque community on the northern outskirts of Bolton was first established in 1835 by Thomas Bazley and Robert Gardner to house workers at their cotton spinning and doubling mill. The mill village rapidly became known as an archetypal model of an industrial community. A co-operative society was established here in 1836, some seven years before the better known example in Rochdale.

Barrow Bridge was visited in 1840 by Benjamin Disraeli, who is said to have incorporated it into his novel *Coningsby* as the village of Millbank. In 1851 Albert, the Prince Consort, paid a visit.

Bazley retired in 1862 and the mill closed in 1877, never to reopen. For a long time Barrow Bridge became known as the Deserted Village; the mill was finally demolished in 1913. Since those times the village has become a very pleasant place to live.

Access

Via Barrow Bridge Road, from the A58 (Moss Bank Way) via either Smithills Croft Road or Moss Lane.

See also the mill village of Eagley, located off the Blackburn Road (A666).

A WAYSIDE CROSS

Affetside Cross

On the western side of the main road, in the centre of the village.

Wayside crosses are a common feature in the UK and many have survived in and around Greater Manchester. Dating from medieval times they were often established by religious houses to guide travellers across moorland areas, and were typically provided at prominent points or at the tops of hills.

This cross, an ancient monument, is located at the side of the Roman road that runs through Affetside known as Watling Street.

This particular Watling Street, constructed in AD 79, ran from Manchester to Ribchester and is not to be confused with the one that ran from London to Wroxeter, near Shrewsbury. Affetside is said to be halfway between London and Edinburgh, and the name is alleged to mean 'half each side'.

Various dates ranging from Roman times to the seventeenth century have been put forward as the date of the cross's construction. It was pulled down in about 1890 by treasure-seekers looking for buried gold and was then re-erected on a new stone base.

The cross is now 'headless' and has a socket at the top of the post where the cross formerly sat. Recently the adjoining land has been laid out as an attractive Millennium Garden.

Close by is the Pack Horse Inn, which contains over the bar the skull of George Wherwell, who executed James, 7th Earl of Derby, at Bolton in 1651 during the Civil War. Later the Royalists took their revenge on Wherwell, a resident of Affetside, and executed him, displaying his head on a pike outside the Pack Horse.

10

CURIOSITIES OF WIGAN

GEORGE FORMBY AND GEORGE ORWELL'S *WIGAN PIER*

Access

The Wigan Pier
complex is just to
the south of the
town centre,
adjacent to the
A49. There are
car parks off
Wallgate, Pottery
Road, and at the
Trencherfield
Mill, via Caroline
Street and St
Thomas Street.

Wigan Pier

Bankes's Pier, to use its historically correct name, was built in 1822 to transfer coal from nearby collieries by rail to the Leeds and Liverpool Canal. It consisted of a tipper mechanism located on a slightly raised and protruding section of the canal bank. Coal wagons would be driven to the end of the line to be stopped by the hooked-up rail ends. The wagon would then be tipped to have its front opened to empty the coal into the waiting barge.

In 1842 the installation was taken over by Squire Meyrick Bankes, who extended the railway to serve more collieries. It is said to have handled up to 1,000 tons of coal a week in the mid-nineteenth century but was closed and removed in 1929 after the closure of the Winstanley and Worsley Mesnes collieries. The photograph above shows a 'cruise' leaving the pier in the early years of the twentieth century.

The present structure is a replica built in the 1980s as part of the ambitious and popular Wigan Pier development.

The name 'Wigan Pier' is said to have been originated by George Formby senior who used it as a music hall joke, but the name was firmly established in the 1930s when George Orwell wrote *The Road to Wigan Pier*.

HORSE ROLLERS

Access

As for Wigan Pier.

Leeds & Liverpool Canal

Located in the heart of the Wigan Pier complex, between 'The Way We Were' and Trencherfield Mill (said to contain the world's largest working mill engine), and underneath the A49 road bridge, are these metal rollers. They were provided to stop the towropes of horse-drawn canal boats from causing grooving in the stonework of the bridge.

BUILT AS A PENANCE FOR A LADY'S BIGAMY

Mab's Cross

This cross, once located on the opposite side of the road, is believed to date from early medieval times. According to legend its name originated in the early fourteenth century.

In 1295 William de Bradshaigh married Mabel de Norreys, heiress of the Haigh estate. After Sir William had been absent so long in the Crusades Mabel took him to be dead, and after a seven-year wait she remarried. Subsequently Sir William returned and killed his successor (in the myth a Welsh knight) at Newton-le-Willows.

As penance for her bigamy Lady Mabel walked barefoot every week, wearing sackcloth and carrying a candle, from Haigh to the Cross and then to the edge of Wigan.

Access

On the eastern side of Standishgate (A49) on the northern side of the town centre.

See also the tomb of Sir William and Lady Mabel in Wigan parish church (open some summer Saturdays).

IN THE CENTRE OF THE TOWN

Stocks & Market Cross, Standish

Access

In front of the sixteenth-century St Wilfrid's Church, just off the A49.

Despite being predominantly an urban county Greater Manchester is not without some of the more traditional curiosities found in the shire counties. Standish's ancient wooden stocks and market cross are good examples.

The market cross here was erected in the fourteenth century and is a Scheduled Ancient Monument. The cross itself was broken off just above the base during the Reformation or the Commonwealth eras, but was restored by Celia Strickland in the early nineteenth century. The adjoining stocks are of medieval origin and were relocated here in the 1890s after being found in a field.

Standish's marketplace was formerly referred to as 'The Town'. In 1998 the historic Well House was rebuilt immediately adjacent to the market cross and stocks. This had been damaged by an American Army vehicle in 1943 and subsequently demolished.

The adjoining St Wilfrid's Church is one of the most interesting in Lancashire. The gatehouse was completed in 1926 as a war memorial and contains on its rear face an effigy of St Wilfrid holding a model of the church, above the entrance gateway.

Other village stocks can be found at St Luke's Church, Lowton, outside Saddleworth Church, in Mottram village and at Warburton in Trafford, where there are also the remains of a market cross.

GREATER MANCHESTER'S ONLY WINDMILL

Windmill, Haigh Country Park

This small windmill, now the only windmill in the county, was built in the late 1840s. It was erected to pump water from two ponds to the Haigh Brewery, established by John Sumner and formerly located behind the Balcarres Arms.

The windmill was small, since the requirements of the brewery were not great, and its surplus water also supplied some other properties on the estate. A windmill was used not only because the running costs were less than those of a steam-driven pump but also because Lord Crawford would not have wanted a smoky chimney in operation so close to his estate and hall.

At some time later the brewery began to use mains water and the need for the windmill ended. The brewery closed shortly before the start of the Second World War and the windmill became derelict thereafter. It was restored in the early 1980s, and again fairly recently.

Access

Via Copperas Lane, off the B5230 at the Balcarres Arms. The windmill is on the left in the fields.

A Reminder of a Civil War Battle

Access

At the junction of Wigan Lane and Monument Street, to the north of Wigan town centre.

Tyldesley Monument, Wigan Lane

This monument was erected in 1679 in memory of a local Cavalier, Sir Thomas Tyldesley, who died at 3 pm on 25 August 1651 at the battle of Wigan Lane, when the Royalist forces under the Earl of Derby were decisively defeated in what was the last battle of the Civil War to be fought in Lancashire.

Sir Thomas, born in 1592, is often claimed to have been the person who caused the first bloodshed of the Civil War, when he shot dead Richard Perceval on 15 July 1642.

During the Civil War Wigan remained loyal to the King, partly on account of the influence of the Earl of Derby, who lived nearby and as a consequence made it his headquarters. Nearby Bolton was for Parliament, however, and the early stages of the Civil War resulted in conflicts between the two towns. Sir Thomas fought in the battle of Edgehill and was knighted in 1643 after showing bravery in the storming of Burton-on-Trent. He also served as Governor of Lichfield.

The battle of Wigan Lane consisted of a series of charges up and down the Lane, with close-quarter cavalry fighting and sniper fire from parliamentary forces hidden in the hedgerows. It is said that Sir Thomas was killed shortly after his horse was shot from under him.

After his death his body was taken to the Tyldesley Chapel in Leigh parish church, where he was buried. A portrait of him hung for many years in Tyldesley Town Hall and now hangs in Leigh Town Hall.

The Monument, which marks the spot where Tyldesley died, was erected in 1679 by one of the officers in the Wigan Lane battle, one Alexander Rigby, who had served as cornet to the Earl of Derby and who by then had become High Sheriff of Lancashire. It was restored by Wigan Corporation in 1886.

THE MOST UNLIKELY-LOOKING VILLAGE GREEN IN ENGLAND

Access

On the south
side of Park
Lane, at Abram
Brow, about half
a mile from the
A673.

Morris Dancing Ground, Abram

This rather nondescript plot of land is where morris dancing was traditionally performed in Abram. No one knows when this plot was first used for this purpose but it is likely to have been the eighteenth century or earlier. At the time such dancing was common in towns and villages of the North-West, but the practice continued longer in Abram than elsewhere.

The land was eventually donated to the people of Abram on condition that the dance, performed here uniquely with a maypole, occurred at regular intervals, reported to be as long as twenty-one years by some sources. The particular version of the dance used at Abram is often called the Abram Circle Dance, and is known among morris dance aficionados around the world.

The tradition seemed to die out with the last dance on 1 July 1901 but it has been revived in the last couple of decades. In 1972, following pressure from enthusiasts keen to revive the dance in its own village, the land was given 'village green' status, and in 1976 it was registered as 'common land'. In May 1984 the land was used for morris dancing again, and it now takes place annually.

Efforts are being made to get the land restored as currently it is probably the most unlikely-looking village green in England.

11

CURIOSITIES THAT HAVE NOW DISAPPEARED

One of the inevitabilities of urban development and redevelopment is that curiosities disappear, particularly when their significance is not appreciated. A few examples follow of curiosities that have all gone from Greater Manchester in the past dozen or so years, although, on a final optimistic note, one of them is being relocated and may have been rebuilt by the time this book appears in print.

Steam Pipes, Rochdale Canal, Manchester

In these energy-efficient days much has been made of the possibilities of CHP (Combined Heat and Power) plants. Manchester, it is claimed, had the first such scheme, and these pipes, complete with expansion loops, which formerly ran along the Rochdale Canal, were part of that scheme. They led from the former power station on Bloom Street built in 1901–2, and took away surplus steam from the generators to supply nearby buildings, including the Palace Theatre.

Although power ceased to be generated at Bloom Street in 1954 the heating system continued, steam being produced by oil-fired boilers. It remained in use until the mid-1990s, when the pipes were removed as part of the general initiative to tidy up the canal where it ran through the city centre.

Medlock Cloughs, Castlefield

This interesting structure was hidden away behind high walls at the southern end of Deansgate at the point where the River Medlock flows into the Bridgewater Canal. The river was used by James Brindley as the main water supply for the Manchester end of the canal. However, water was not always required by the canal, and from 1838 this self-tilting weir diverted surplus water, when the water in the canal reached a certain height, into a 500yd culvert that ran beneath the canal complex at Castlefield and deposited the water into the old river line west of Potato Wharf.

The weir was removed in the early 1990s, although it had been out of use for some time before then.

Former National Westminster Bank, 35 King Street

There were formerly two branches of the NatWest on King Street. This one, quaintly referred to as the Lloyd Entwisle Office, had been in use as a bank since 1788, and two plaques outside recorded the names of the various banking companies that had occupied it since then. Inside was a small display of old banking equipment and documentation.

The building was completely redeveloped in the 1990s, and although the frontage has been retained it is no longer a bank.

Camouflaged Hangar, Manchester Airport

Some forty-five years after it was erected and last painted this aircraft hangar near to Avro Way, known at the airport as Hangar 5, still retained its Second World War camouflage, up to its demolition in the early 1990s.

Aries Coach, Oldham Road, Rochdale

This genuine Pullman coach, built in 1952 by the Pullman Company, was used as a restaurant at the Yew Tree pub, adjacent to the M62 motorway. It was formerly in use on the Southern Region of British Railways and was withdrawn from service in 1967. Two years later it was brought to the pub by the enterprising landlord of the time.

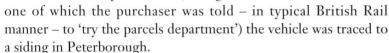

British Rail were to have delivered it to Rochdale by rail but the coach was somehow 'lost' on the way, and after some frantic phone calls (during one of which the purchaser was told – in typical British Rail manner – to 'try the parcels department') the vehicle was traced to a siding in Peterborough.

The coach arrived on its site with tremendous press and public interest and was cheered on its way by the assembled local Licensed Victuallers Association. Originally intended to be a 'five-year novelty', it lasted in fact until the late 1990s.

This One has Gone but is Returning: Dovecote, Rifle Road, Sale

This dovecote, formerly located half-buried on a traffic roundabout on the M60 motorway, was the sole surviving structure of Sale Old Hall. The dovecote was built in about 1885 by local architect Thomas Worthington for a relative of his who lived at the Hall.

The motorway was built in the early 1970s, and over the years the authorities have blown 'hot and cold' over whether to do something about the dovecote. Various proposals were mooted for its relocation, but none was implemented until plans to further widen the motorway were made a couple of years ago. The dovecote has now been taken apart but (at the time of writing) should be reappearing soon in a new location in Walkden Gardens, Sale.

INDEX

Adams, Norman 13
Addy, Mark 64
Affetside Cross 174
Aiggin Stone, Blackstone Edge 154
Ainsworth, Harrison 20
Air Raid Shelters, Stockport 96, 97
Alan Turing statue 31, 32
Albert Memorial 10
Alexandra Park, Oldham 134
Aries coach, Rochdale 190
ancient monuments 90, 180
arches 28–9, 58, 118
Ardernes (of Bredbury) 95
Ashley Grange 51
Assheton, Lord Richard 146
Astley Green Colliery 166

Bankes, Squire Meyrick 176–7
banks 95, 188–9
Barrow Bridge village 173
Barry, Charles 169
Barton Arcade 17
Barton, Robert 172
Barton Swing Aqueduct 87
Bazley, Thomas 173
beacons 117
Beckett, Wilf 34
Belle Vue Jail 58
Blackstone Edge, Littleborough 153–4
Bloody footprint, Smithills Hall, Bolton 172
Boars Head Inn 146
Bob's Lane Ferry, Partington 88
Bonehill 25
Boyle, Sir Edward 47
Bradbury, William and Thomas 139
Bradshaigh, William de 179
bridges and viaducts 58, 92, 105, 147
Bridgewater, Duke of 68, 71, 72
Bridgewater Hall 36
Bridgewater Pebble 36
Brierley, Ben 115
Brierley, Cllr Jackson 134
Brierley, Lewis 128
Brindley, James 38, 87, 187
Britannia Hotel 33, 34
Broadway Garden Village, 114
Brooks Drive, Hale and Timperley 89
Brooks family 89

Brown, Ford Madox 45
Brumby, Robert 44
Buckton Castle, Carrbrook 123
Bull's Head datestone, Mottram 127
Byrom, John 18, 66

Calico Printers Association 35
camouflaged hangar, Manchester Airport 189
canals 31, 38, 68, 87, 104, 106, 108, 115, 140, 150, 168, 176, 186, 187
Castlefield 37, 144
Castle Hill, Bowdon 90
castles 123
Castleshaw Roman Fort 144
cemeteries 113
Central Reference Library 20
Chadkirk Chapel, Romiley 109
Champneys, Basil 20
Charlton, Sir Bobby 85
Chartism 56, 118
'Cheeryble Brothers' 159
Chester, Earl of 123
Chetham, Sir Humphrey 20
Chetham's Library, Hospital and School 20
Chinatown 28, 31, 46
Chinese Arch 28
Chorltonville 50
churches and chapels 12, 20, 22, 23, 44, 45, 47, 51, 53, 56, 72, 98, 99, 104, 112, 127, 128, 132, 137, 146, 164, 169, 179
Church, Edwin 51
Churchgate Cross, Bolton 167
'Circus, The' 30
Clinch, Fr Dennis 13
clocks 11, 72–3, 85, 93, 157
Cobden, Richard 60
colleges and universities 32, 45, 47, 56
Collier, John ('Tim Bobbin') 147
collieries 68, 116, 166
column capitals, Stockport 98
Coningsby 173
conservation areas 112, 171
Cotton Trading Boards, Royal Exchange 14
Co-operative Movement, Rochdale 148–9

Co-operative Union 148
Coronation Street set 39
Cotterill Clough 54
country parks 110, 150–1, 181
Coward, T.A. 54
Crawford, Lord 181
Crime Lake, Daisy Nook 115
Crompton, Samuel 171
Crossland, W.H. 147
Crown Pole, Mottram 126
'Curry Mile', Rusholme 46

Dawson, J.H. 50
Defoe, Daniel 153
Delph, Worsley 68–9
Dovecote, Rifle Road, Sale 190
Drinking trough, Withington 48

earthworks 59, 90, 100, 123, 144
East Lancashire Railway 160
Eaton, John 117
Ellenroad Engine House 166
Ellesmere, Earl of 37, 70, 74
Ellesmere Memorial, Worsley 74
Elms, The, Mottram 129
Engels, Frederick 20
engines 166
Estate Railway, Trafford Park 84
Etherow Country Park 108

Failsworth Pole 136
Fairbottom Bobs 116
Fairfield Moravian Settlement 112
farms and agricultural buildings 52, 75–6, 163, 164
Fenian Arch 58
First Church of Christ, Scientist, Victoria Park 45
Firwood Fold, Bolton 171
Fletcher, Ellis 67
Fletcher's Folly, Clifton Country Park 67
follies 61, 67
Ford, Henry 116
Formby, George 177
fountains 10, 71
Frog Stone, Mottram 130

gardens 28, 55, 78
garden suburbs 114

Gardner, Robert 173
gas lamp, Delph 142
gateways 28, 78, 118
Geological Garden 44
George III 126
glacial boulder, Rosehill,
  Northenden 51
Goadsby, Thomas 10
Goodwin, Francis 60
Granada TV 39
Grant, William and Daniel 159
Grants Tower 159
Great Underbank Hall, Stockport
  95
Greswell, Revd William Parr
  124
'Grey Horse' 30
Grocers' Warehouse 38
Guardian telephone exchange 27

Hallé, Charles 45
Hallé Orchestra 36
Handy's Circus 30
hanging bridge/ditch 22, 66
Hartshead Pike, Ashton 117
Harwood, George 167
headstone from Mellor Mill,
  Marple 103
Hearse House, Saddleworth 137
Heathcote & Brown 78–9
heating systems 186
Heaton Park Tramway 62
heritage centres 94
Hick Hargreaves & Co. Ltd 166
Hidden Gem 12
Hitler, Adolf 147
Holland, Sir Richard 124
Hollings College 47
Hollingworth Lake 150–1
Holloway, Anthony 23
Horse and foot tunnels, Posset
  Bridge, Marple 105
Horse rollers, Leeds & Liverpool
  Canal, Wigan 178
hotels 33–4
houses and halls 61, 66, 95, 112,
  114, 129, 181
Howard, Ebenezer 52
Howarth, Joseph 135
Huntington, John 25
Hughes, Glyn 31
Hulme's Bridge Ferry, Davyhulme
  88
Hus, John 112–13
Hyde Road 58
Hydes Cross 20

IRA bomb 15, 17, 19, 36

Jennings, J.A. 151
John Rylands Library 20
Judge, Jack 119
Judges Bar, Stalybridge 119

Kay Monument, Bury 158
Kenworthy, Catherine 132
Kenworthy Memorial, Mossley 132
Kenyon, Sir William & Co. 125
Kersal Cell 66
Kershaw, Walter 81
King of Tonga 139
Knob Hall Gardens 52
Knowles, Joshua 163

Ladysmith Barracks, Ashton 118
lakes 82, 115, 150
lamp posts 126, 142, 149
Lancashire & Yorkshire Railway 24
La Trobe, Revd Benjamin 113
Levenshulme Antiques
  Village/Hypermarket 55
Lewis, Terry MP 76
libraries 20
Lime Kilns, Marple 106–7
listed buildings 112
Liverpool & Manchester Railway 40
Liverpool Road station 40
Longdendale, Lord of 123
Lowry, L.S. 115, 129

Mab's Cross, Wigan 131, 179
Manchester Airport 36, 53, 189
Manchester Blitz 34, 44
Manchester Metropolitan
  University 45, 47
Manchester Museum 44, 54
Manchester Town Hall 10, 26, 60
Manchester Transport Museum
  Society 62
Manchester Ship Canal 44, 65, 88,
  90
Manchester University 32, 56
Mark Addy's Bridge 64
Marks & Spencer 16, 17
market crosses 180
markets 25
Marsh, Revd George 172
Martyrs Memorial 58
Marx, Karl 20
Maxwell & Tuke 157
Mechanics' Institute 30
Medlock Cloughs, Castlefield 187
Memorial Garden, Heyhead 53

memorials 10, 24, 33, 51, 53–4, 71,
  74, 75, 85, 132, 135, 138, 146,
  159, 161, 182–3
Middleton Archers 146
milepost, A62, Delph 143
Millbank 173
Mill engine, Bolton 166
mills 102, 108, 166
Mitchell Gardens 52
monastic buildings 66, 104
montage, St Augustine's Church
  44
monuments 10–11, 182
morris dancing ground, Abram 184
Morrison, Kerry 32
Mosley, Sir Oswald 14
Mottram parish church 128
Mottram Watchers 128
Mount Sion Bleach Works 168
Munich Clock 85
museums 26, 44, 54, 148

National Museum of Labour
  History 26
National Westminster Bank
  (former), Manchester 188–9
New Bailey Jail 58
Newton Hall, Hyde 125
Nicholas Nickleby 159
Nichols, John Joel & J.N. & Co.
  32
Nicko Ditch 59
Norreys, Mabel de 179
Nuttall, F.M. & H. 157
Nuttall Hall Farm 159
Nuttall, Harry 50

Observatory, Alexandra Park,
  Oldham 134
offices 14, 35
Ogden, George 137
Old Blind Joe, Alexandra Park,
  Oldham 135
Oldknow, Samuel 103, 105, 106
Old Reading Room, Chetham's
  Library 20
Old Smithfield Market 25
Old Toll Gates, Victoria Park 42
Old Town Hall frontage, Heaton
  Park 60–1
Old Town Hall, Stockport Road,
  Levenshulme 55
Old Wellington Inn 18
Orwell, George 177

Packet Steps, Worsley 70

Pack Horse Inn, Affetside 174
Park Bridge, Ashton 116
Parker, Barry 52
parks 11, 59, 60, 61, 67, 86, 109, 134–5
Pear New Mill, Bredbury 102
Peel Moat, Heaton Moor 100
Peel, Sir Robert 159, 161
Peel Tower, Holcombe Brook 161
Perceval, Richard 182
Pevsner, Nikolaus 45
'Pink' Manchester 31, 32
Plague Stones, Gorse Hill Park, Stretford 86
plaques 34, 55, 120, 137
poles 126, 136
Polly the pig 75
Pomona Gardens 65
Portico Library 20
Posset Bridge, Marple 105
post-boxes 16, 148–9
Pot Church 47
Pots and Pans Stone, Greenfield 138
Princess Alexandra 117
Prince of Wales 117
public houses 30, 64, 75, 93, 105, 119, 121, 127, 146, 156, 162, 174
Pugin, A.W. 13
Pump House Museum 26
pumping stations 26

Queen Elizabeth II 117
Queen Victoria 70, 79
Q Inn, Stalybridge 122

Radcliffe, James 164
Radcliffe Tower 164
railways 24, 51, 84, 92, 160
railway stations 24, 40, 122, 160
Rakewood Viaduct 151
Ramsbottom, Jim 64
Regional War Room, Cheadle 101
reservoirs 152
Rigby, Alexander 182
Ringley, Mock Mayor of 169
Ringley Tower 169
rivers 64
Rochdale Town Hall 147
Rocher New Pit 116
Roman remains 37, 100, 144, 153
Roman road, Blackstone Edge 153
Roman wall, Castlefield 37
Rosehill 51
Roving Bridge, canal junction, Marple 104
Round House, Every Street, Ancoats 56

Royal Exchange/Royal Exchange Theatre 14

St George's Church, Mossley 132
St James's Buildings/Hall 35
St John Street 39
St Lawrence's Church, Denton 124
St Leonard's Church, Middleton 146
St Mark's Church, Worsley 72
St Michael & All Angels Church, Mottram 128
schools 113
Scolefield, James 56
sculpture 36, 44
secret establishments 27, 101
Sellars, J.H. 114
Shambles, The 18
Sharstone 51
Shaw, John 18
Shirley Institute 49
signpost, Bradshaw 170
Sinclairs Oyster Bar 18
Smithfield Craft Centre 75
Smith, Hedley 114
Smithills Hall, Bolton 172
Staircase Café, Stockport 94
statues 10–11
Staveleigh, Sir Ralph de 128, 131
Standedge canal tunnel 140
steam crane, Manchester, Bolton & Bury Canal 168
steam pipes, Rochdale Canal, Manchester 186
Stevens, Marshall 80
Stockport Grammar School 94
Stockport Viaduct 92
stocks and market cross, Standish 180
Sumner, John 181

Tarquin 86
Taylor, James 137
Taylor, John 49
telephone exchanges 27
theatres and cinemas 14, 35, 92, 119–20, 186
Thirlmere Fountain 10
Thirteenth Cheshire Rifleman Inn, Stalybridge 121
Toad Lane Museum 148
'Toasted Cheese Club' 156
'Toastrack Building', Fallowfield 47
toll-gates 42–3, 90
Tootal 35
Tottington Dungeon 162
tourist and visitor centres 11, 23
Tower Court and Farm 163

towers 74, 117, 164, 169, 170
Towers, the, Didsbury 49
town halls 10, 11, 55, 99, 147
Trafford Park entrance mural 80
Trafford Park Lake 82–3
Trahearne, Margaret 23
tramways 36, 62, 108
Trencherfield Mill 166
tunnels 140–1
Two Tubs, Bury 156
Tyldesley, Sir Thomas 182

Vernon, Horace 120
Victoria Park 42, 45
Victoria station 24
Vimto sculpture, Manchester 32
Vowles, W.J. 50

Wakes week holidays 124
'Wall of History', Waterworth Reservoir, Rochdale 152
Wallwork, Nathan 169
Warburton Toll-Bridge 90
war memorials 24, 146
warehouses 33
Warren, Tony 39
Watch Hill, Bowdon 90
Water Street pumping station 26
Watkin, Sir Edward 51
Watling Street 174
Watts, James 32, 53
Watts Warehouse 32
wayside crosses 154, 174, 179
Webb, Captain 151
Wellington, Duke of 40
Wesley, John 167
Wherwell, George 174
White City entrance, Old Trafford 78, 86
Whitehead clock tower 157
Whitehead, Henry and Walter 157, 158
White Stone, Mottram 131
widest bridge, Rochdale 147
Wigan Pier 176
Williams, Sir Edward Leader 87
Williams, Harry 120
windmill, Haigh Country Park 181
Winter, Jacob 93
Winter's Clockhouse 93
Woden Street footbridge 65
Wood, Edgar 45, 61, 114
Worthington, Thomas 10
Wythenshawe estate 52

Yeoman Hey and Bills-O-Jacks Plantations, Greenfield 139